Dark Victory

Wisconsin/Warner Bros. Screenplay Series

Editorial Board

Dudley Andrew
Tino Balio, *General Editor*
John G. Cawelti
John Fell

Dark Victory

Edited with an introduction by

Bernard F. Dick

Published for the Wisconsin Center for Film and Theater Research by
The University of Wisconsin Press

Published 1981

The University of Wisconsin Press
114 North Murray Street
Madison, Wisconsin 53715

The University of Wisconsin Press, Ltd.
1 Gower Street
London WC1E 6HA, England

Copyright © 1981
The Board of Regents of the University of Wisconsin System
All rights reserved

First printing

Printed in the United States of America

For LC CIP information see the colophon

ISBN 0-299-08760-3 cloth; 0-299-08764-6 paper

Publication of this volume has been assisted by a grant from
The Brittingham Fund, Inc.

Contents

Foreword   7
   Tino Balio

Introduction: The Fine Art of Dying   9
   Bernard F. Dick

Illustrations   43

Dark Victory   55

Notes to the Screenplay   206

Production Credits   211

Cast   212

Inventory   213

Foreword

In donating the Warner Film Library to the Wisconsin Center for Film and Theater Research in 1969, along with the RKO and Monogram film libraries and UA corporate records, United Artists created a truly great resource for the study of American film. Acquired by United Artists in 1957, during a period when the major studios sold off their films for use on television, the Warner library is by far the richest portion of the gift, containing eight hundred sound features, fifteen hundred short subjects, nineteen thousand still negatives, legal files, and press books, in addition to screenplays for the bulk of the Warner Brothers product from 1930 to 1950. For the purposes of this project, the company has granted the Center whatever publication rights it holds to the Warner films. In so doing, UA has provided the Center another opportunity to advance the cause of film scholarship.

Our goal in publishing these Warner Brothers screenplays is to explicate the art of screenwriting during the thirties and forties, the so-called Golden Age of Hollywood. In preparing a critical introduction and annotating the screenplay, the editor of each volume is asked to cover such topics as the development of the screenplay from its source to the final shooting script, differences between the final shooting script and the release print, production information, exploitation and critical reception of the film, its historical importance, its directorial style, and its position within the genre. He is also encouraged to go beyond these guidelines to incorporate supplemental information concerning the studio system of motion picture production.

We could set such an ambitious goal because of the richness of the script files in the Warner Film Library. For many film titles, the files might contain the property (novel, play, short story, or original story idea), research materials, variant drafts of scripts

Foreword

(from story outline to treatment to shooting script), post-production items such as press books and dialogue continuities, and legal records (details of the acquisition of the property, copyright registration, and contracts with actors and directors). Editors of the Wisconsin/Warner Bros. Screenplay Series receive copies of all the materials, along with prints of the films (the most authoritative ones available for reference purposes), to use in preparing the introductions and annotating the final shooting scripts.

In the process of preparing the screenplays for publication, typographical errors were corrected, punctuation and capitalization were modernized, and the format was redesigned to facilitate readability.

Unless otherwise specified, the photographs are frame enlargements taken from a 35-mm print of the film provided by United Artists.

In 1977 Warner Brothers donated the company's production records and distribution records to the University of Southern California and Princeton University, respectively. These materials are now available to researchers and complement the contents of the Warner Film Library donated to the Center by United Artists.

Tino Balio
General Editor

Introduction: *The Fine Art of Dying*

Bernard F. Dick

Like all films, Dark Victory has a history that is factual, anecdotal, and mythical. As for facts, it originated as an unsuccessful play by George Brewer, Jr., and Bertram Bloch that starred Tallulah Bankhead and ran for fifty-one performances during the 1934–35 Broadway season. The drama had a history of rewrites, dropped options, and title changes; copyrighted in 1932 as *In Time's Course*, it then became *No More Day*, *Days without End*, and finally *Dark Victory*. For three years the producers tried to interest Bankhead in appearing in it, and the actress claimed to have read at least six versions of the script, the final one purportedly containing revisions by Maxwell Anderson, who was a member of the production team that brought *Dark Victory* to the stage of the Plymouth theater on November 7, 1934.[1]

Those who remember Tallulah Bankhead as the star of radio's *The Big Show* or of such films as *Lifeboat* (1944) and *A Royal Scandal* (1945) might find it difficult to imagine her as Judith Traherne, a Long Island heiress who develops a brain tumor and learns to accept death with the help of a surgeon who functions as friend, priest, and finally husband. Yet Brooks Atkinson of the *New York Times* dismissed neither Bankhead nor the play, noting that the actress brought an "intuitive stage intelligence" to the part and that the play itself was "not destitute of quality" (November 10, 1934). Still, Atkinson could not give the drama his unqualified approval; although he admired the first act, he had to admit that once the playwrights gave Judith six months to

---

1. Tallulah Bankhead, *Tallulah: My Autobiography* (New York: Harper, 1952), pp. 214–15.

Introduction

live, they doomed the play as well, condemning it to death by sententiousness.

Atkinson was correct; it was not an inferior play, merely an undistinguished one. Essentially, *Dark Victory* was a drawing room tragedy like Samson Raphaelson's *Hilda Crane* (1950), unable to divorce itself from a setting that conjured up cocktails and canapés. Thus someone would have to toss off an occasional witticism to keep the gloom from settling over the furniture. But the attempts at wit were feeble ("Your magnificent mistress has cut her name in the left breast of the Muse of History," a character exclaims at one point), and *Dark Victory* became the reverse of Philip Barry's *Holiday* (1928) in which the madcap heiress was now terminally ill and the only way to live happily ever after was in the afterlife.

What fails on the stage often succeeds on the screen. Edward Childs Carpenter's forgotten *Connie Goes Home* (1923) became Billy Wilder's *The Major and the Minor* (1942); Elmer Harris's *Johnny Belinda* (1940) is known through the 1948 movie version that won Jane Wyman an Oscar. David O. Selznick, a vice president at Metro-Goldwyn-Mayer from 1933 to 1935, sensed that *Dark Victory* would be an ideal vehicle for Greta Garbo. It is impossible, however, to imagine MGM's making a film about a woman dying of a brain tumor without deleting all references to the nature of the disease and making the character so insufferably noble that women would want a similar affliction for themselves. On January 7, 1935, Selznick fired off one of his famous memos to Garbo, urging her to forget *Anna Karenina* and do the "modern" *Dark Victory* with Fredric March, who was tired of costume dramas and wanted to wear a suit again.[2] If the memo is accurate, other studios were vying for the screen rights, and Katharine Hepburn was seriously interested in playing the lead. Although it is tempting to contemplate a *Dark Victory* with Garbo and March speaking Philip Barry's dialogue as Selznick had hoped, one suspects it would have been as unmemorable as a *Casablanca* with Dennis Morgan, Ronald Reagan, and Ann

---

2. *Memo from David O. Selznick*, ed. Rudy Behlmer (New York: Viking, 1972), pp. 75–77.

Introduction

Sheridan or a *High Sierra* with George Raft. At any rate, Garbo ended up doing *Anna Karenina* (1935) with March as Vronsky. March got his change of wardrobe in *The Dark Angel* (1935), and Garbo made her fatal illness film a year later when she expired, beautifully coiffured and ethereally lit, in *Camille* (1936), which was more suited to her dark romanticism.

Selznick, however, had not abandoned hope. After founding his own company, Selznick International, he purchased the screen rights early in 1936 for $18,500 (not $50,000 as commonly thought), hired Rachel Crothers to write the screenplay, and had Janet Gaynor or Carole Lombard in mind for the lead. One can only imagine the lustrous femininity Lombard would have brought to the role of Judith. But Lombard did *Nothing Sacred* (1937) for Selznick, and Gaynor, *A Star Is Born* (1937). As 1938 began *Dark Victory* was still unfilmed, although four screenplays had been written; by the end of the year, it had been made—but not by Selznick.

Now the facts move into soft focus as *Dark Victory* moves from Selznick International to Warner Brothers. There are two accounts of how Warners acquired *Dark Victory*; while they do not contradict each other, they do not exactly complement each other either. The better documented version is Casey Robinson's; the more familiar is Bette Davis's.[3]

In 1935 Casey Robinson, after scoring a personal success with his script for *Captain Blood* (1935), happened to be in New York looking for screenplay material when his agent, Leland Hayward, called his attention to *Dark Victory*. Robinson read the play in a hot bath, and suddenly "the whole concept of the picture, the whole structure" materialized as if in an epiphany. Upon his return to Los Angeles, he told Hal Wallis, then executive producer at Warners, about the play. Although Wallis was disturbed by the cancer theme, he was willing to make the picture

---

3. Robinson's version can be found in "Elizabethan Awakening in Store for Cinema Art," *Los Angeles Times*, April 7, 1968, Calendar, p. 16; "Casey Robinson on *Dark Victory*," *Australian Journal of Screen Theory*, 4 (1978), 5–10; Joel Greenberg, "Writing for the Movies: Casey Robinson," *Focus on Film*, 32 (April 1979), 11–12. Davis's is in her autobiography, *The Lonely Life* (New York: G. P. Putnam, 1962), p. 224.

Introduction

until he discovered that Selznick owned the rights. For three years Robinson hoped Selznick would never make *Dark Victory*. In June 1938, his wish came true when Selznick sold the rights to Warners for $27,500—not for the same mythical $50,000 as some accounts have it. Selznick would hardly miss the chance to make a profit.

From her autobiography, one would think Bette Davis was solely responsible for Warners' making *Dark Victory*. She claims to have "peddled" the property to every producer on the lot, finally managing to interest David Lewis, the associate producer of her latest film, *The Sisters* (1938). Having produced *Camille* at MGM, Lewis was also sympathetic to the subject matter. Davis and Lewis then enlisted the support of Edmund Goulding, who had directed Davis in *That Certain Woman* (1937). "Between the three of us we got Mr. Warner to buy the property," Davis recalls in *The Lonely Life*. Because *Jezebel* was grossing well, Warner told Wallis he would purchase *Dark Victory* for Davis: "Just get her off my back," he begged.[4]

Alternate versions are common in history; they are inevitable in film history, which frequently must draw on memoirs and interviews. Robinson's version does not invalidate Davis's; the trio may well have been campaigning to make the film, and Davis may well have been pestering Warner. Nor does Davis's version negate Robinson's; it simply ignores his contribution to the film.

If Robinson is to be believed, and except for a few details there is no reason why he should not be, the maneuvers were more complex than Davis realized. Robinson maintains that what finally convinced Warner was the dual prospect of satisfying a commitment to Davis and buying a property that Selznick was unable to film because of script problems that Robinson felt could be solved. Moreover, Robinson had been entrusted with the task of finding a suitable script for Davis. Thus, when Robinson writes that it was he who told Davis about *Dark Victory* and

---

4. Program Notes for the Hal B. Wallis Retrospective at Los Angeles County Museum of Art (July 26, 1974); see also Whitney Stine, *Mother Goddam: The Story of the Career of Bette Davis* (New York: Hawthorn, 1974), pp. 105–14.

Introduction

who made the overtures to David Lewis, one tends to believe him.

Unfortunately, Robinson takes credit for more than he should. Believing that Davis was being masculinized by a studio that favored its actors at the expense of its actresses, Robinson planned to restore her femininity. Ignoring the four scripts that had been prepared for Selznick, he fashioned his own, which led him to claim that "for the first time I was able to present Miss Davis in a truly feminine role which launched her into that orbit of success at the box office which her talent so richly deserved."[5] One wonders how Jack Warner would have responded to this Pygmalion-like boast since it was Warner who claims to have transformed a "sometimes bland and not beautiful little girl into a great artist."[6]

Warners may have turned Davis over to Robinson, as he maintains, but his perception of Davis's screen image is faulty. It is inaccurate to say that Warners masculinized Davis. Admittedly, Warners was a more "masculine" studio than, say, Paramount. Yet Warners produced a number of films that portrayed women in an astonishing variety of occupations: as lawyers (*Scarlet Pages*, 1930; *The Law in Her Hands*, 1936); copywriters (*Big Business Girl*, 1931); reporters (*Front Page Woman*, 1935; *Smart Blonde*, 1937; *Off the Record*, 1939); actresses (*I Found Stella Parish*, 1935; *Dangerous*, 1936); surgeons (*Mary Stevens, M.D.*, 1933; *King of the Underworld*, 1939); models (*The Reckless Hour*, 1931); nurses (*Registered Nurse*, 1934; *The White Angel*, 1936). Davis made many films of this type herself, running the gamut from secretaries (*Three on a Match*, 1932) to ex-molls who became mothers (*That Certain Woman*). Since the Warners woman was an amalgam of guts and glamour, she was tougher and more resilient than the chaise longue beauties of MGM. But resilience and masculinity are not synonymous; Bette Davis and Warner Brothers are.

Like any film of the studio years, *Dark Victory* becomes more meaningful when placed within the double context of the star's

5. *Los Angeles Times*, April 7, 1968, Calendar, p. 16.
6. Jack L. Warner with Dean Jennings, *My First Hundred Years in Hollywood* (New York: Random House, 1964), p. 206.

Introduction

career and the studio's history. Davis admits that Judith Traherne was her favorite role and the public's as well; if this is the case, then her success in the role reflects on both Bette Davis and Warner Brothers, for from 1931 to the end of the 1940s, they were synonymous.

Yet it was one of the stormiest relationships that ever existed between a studio and its star; graphically, it would resemble a fever chart. Davis would no sooner make one good film than she would be assigned to a series of poor ones. As if to punish her for making *Of Human Bondage* (1934) on loanout at RKO because she could not find a decent script at her own studio, Warners released *Housewife* (1934) immediately after her triumph as Maugham's Mildred Rogers. After *Dangerous* and *The Petrified Forest* came *The Golden Arrow* and *Satan Met a Lady* (all 1936), which left her "unhappy, unfulfilled."

Fulfillment came with *Marked Woman* (1937) and *Jezebel* (1938), interspersed with *Kid Galahad*, *It's Love I'm After*, and *That Certain Woman* (all 1937)—less fulfilling, perhaps, but by no means embarrassing. Just when she thought the pattern of one mediocrity for every masterpiece had been altered, she was told she would follow *Jezebel* with *Comet over Broadway* (which, mercifully, was never made). She refused. Although it meant losing twenty-five hundred dollars a week, Davis went on suspension in April 1938, hoping to force the studio to come up with a role suited to her talents. By the end of April, Davis and Warners had resolved their differences, and *The Sisters* went into production, but it was a stopgap measure. As yet there was no mention of *Dark Victory*; the press quoted Davis as saying she would be interested in appearing opposite Paul Muni in either *Juárez* or *The Sea Wolf*. The former came to pass in 1939; the latter featured Edward G. Robinson and Ida Lupino in 1941.

During the spring of 1938, there must have been considerable behind-the-scenes activity. One can imagine a beleaguered Jack Warner, a harassed Hal Wallis, a determined Bette Davis, and an ensemble playing contrapuntal variations on *Dark Victory* as if it had become a mad fugue. Given Hurricane Bette's temperament and her refusal to atone for *Jezebel* by doing schlock, it is perfectly conceivable that Robinson was instructed to find a

Introduction

script for her. Perhaps he thought the time had come for Warners to reconsider *Dark Victory*. Then, too, one should not ignore Wallis's role. Although Wallis does not discuss *Dark Victory* in his autobiography, *Starmaker* (1980), the memos reprinted in the book make it clear that he took an active part in any film he produced. He may have concluded that Selznick would not hold on to a property unless he thought it had screen potential; maybe all *Dark Victory* needed was the right approach and the right actress.

Wallis may have agreed that it was the right time for *Dark Victory*, but for a different reason. MGM's *Camille*, Goldwyn's *Stella Dallas* remake, and Selznick's *A Star Is Born* had all been successful woman's films. Warners could score a coup with the definitive woman's film—the first of a kind which, like any first, would entail a risk but one that seemed worth taking. Whatever the case, it was not coincidental that on June 2, 1938, Warners bought *Dark Victory* from Selznick and that Robinson had the first draft ready a month later. By mid August, the trade papers were carrying production announcements, and in October *Dark Victory* went before the cameras.

With *Dark Victory*, it was not simply a question of Warners' tackling a controversial subject; the studio had done that in the past. It was a matter of tackling a subject that, if handled superficially, would make cancer a romantic malady and, if treated dispassionately, would make it nature's scourge. In terminal illness, the middle ground is hard to find. The play never found it, although, to their credit, Brewer and Bloch did not flinch from using terms like "glioma" and "amblyopia." Robinson retained these words in the Screenplay, working explanations into the dialogue the way a skillful teacher defines a difficult term without letting the class think a definition has been given. One of the most dramatic moments in the film occurs when Judith comes upon her own medical file and reads the phrase "Prognosis Negative." In the Outline, someone had queried "prognosis," implying that it was too technical for the average moviegoer. Judith asks Nurse Wainwright for a definition, not because she does not know the meaning but because she has inferred the meaning and wants proof that her inference was correct, no matter what the consequences. Robinson may have been anticipating a similar reaction from members of the audience who also intuited the meaning and wanted their assumption confirmed.

"Prognosis" was a minor consideration compared with the advertising campaign that would be required to sell the film to the public. As Geraldine Fitzgerald states, "No one was optimistic about its acceptance at the box office; we all thought the subject matter would 'do it in.'"[7] Thus one would hardly expect Warners to advertise *Dark Victory* as a movie about brain cancer. What one saw in the Prevues of Coming Attractions at the local theater was a montage of shots of Davis labeled "Reckless," "Romantic," "Defiant." Since Prevues rarely told anything about the plot, the film seemed to be about a woman and "the shadow that stood between her and every man she loved." It also seemed to be aimed at what *Variety* would call the "femme trade" since it was touted as "the love story no woman will ever forget."

To keep women from forgetting, the press book recommended various promotional gimmicks, including a newspaper ad in the form of a "Dear Madam" letter from the management encouraging female patrons to support "one of the really worthwhile motion pictures of this or any other year"; a *Dark Victory* essay contest in which women would describe their own "dark victory"; a designing contest for the woman's page in which contestants would be invited to design *Dark Victory* apparel; a *Dark Victory* makeup chart with suggestions for the Davis-type light blonde and the Fitzgerald-type brunette.

Since Davis had just won her second Oscar, for *Jezebel*, the publicity naturally centered on her. Davis lookalike contests were recommended; mats for a Bette Davis movie quiz in the local paper were available from Warners for seventy-five cents; the comment cards had Davis's picture on them and could be used as postcards that the patrons would address and the management would mail at its own expense. Although the plot

---

7. Fitzgerald to Dick, August 19, 1980.

Introduction

summaries in the press book did not gloss over the fact that the film was a tragedy, they also did not mention that it dealt with cancer. In a newspaper release, Judith was described as the "victim of a mysterious malady."

The film dispelled the mystery of the malady, as did the newspaper and magazine reviews, with *Life* and *The New Yorker* specifically calling it a brain tumor. While Davis was unanimously praised, the film itself received reviews ranging from good to ecstatic. Generally, the critics respected *Dark Victory*, although it was the kind of film that would arouse ambivalence in reviewers who knew it was not the standard "weepie" but could not explain why. *Variety* (March 7, 1939) concluded an enthusiastic notice with a prediction that the film would attract "the femme trade that delights in long and lusty weeps." Although *Newsweek* (April 24, 1939) believed that without Davis *Dark Victory* "would only be a minor victory of screen over stage," it was impressed with Goulding's "sensitive" direction and the way the film "builds up to its poignant conclusion with cumulative power." On the other hand, *Redbook* and *Time* did not vacillate; *Redbook* named it Picture of the Month, and *Time* (May 1, 1939) curbed its usual cynicism long enough to call it the movies' equivalent of the Rolls-Royce, praising Goulding's "delicate" direction and commending Davis on making the film "moving but not morbid."

However, it was Frank S. Nugent of the *New York Times* (April 21, 1939) who best articulated what most reviewers felt about a movie that seemed to be a woman's film but ultimately transcended that category. Nugent, who was indifferent to *Jezebel*, lauded *Dark Victory* for its refusal to sink into bathos or manipulate its audience. He located the source of the film's integrity in the honesty of the performances and an overall craftsmanship in which artifice and pretense had no place.

Life (April 24, 1939) was so impressed by *Dark Victory*'s unpretentiousness that it used the film as an example of how a major movie could be made for $800,000, arguing that studio economics are better illustrated by a film "handsomely but not elaborately done" than by a "super-spectacle." Since *Life* could

Introduction

not reproduce an official budget, it "worked out"[8] its own, breaking down the $800,000 into the following categories and their approximate costs:

Story and Script	$ 85,000
Actors' and Directors' Salaries	225,000
Scenery and Lighting	100,000
Costumes and Make-up	25,000
Film	15,000
Studio Overhead (taxes, insurance, clerical expenses, legal fees, research, producer's salary)	200,000
Miscellany (publicity, sound operations, music, properties, incidental labor, travel, meals)	150,000

The absence of excess that characterized the budget extended to the entire film, from the classically constructed screenplay to an ideal length of 106 minutes. Jack Warner may have wondered, "Who is going to want to see a picture about a girl who dies?" as Davis states in her autobiography. But the "girl" was Bette Davis, the epitome of the Warner Brothers woman and the ultimate paradox: patrician and proletarian, vulnerable and immune.

The Davis Woman

Davis's screen persona is so complex that it would require a New England cubist to capture all of its facets as well as its peculiarly American character. In the absence of such an artist, one will settle for a retrospective, but it must be a complete one. For if Davis's films were ever shown chronologically, they would reveal the face of the anima in its transcendent beauty

---

8. "Worked out" is the crucial phrase in the article. Warners obviously gave *Life* the $800,000 figure and a general idea of what certain aspects of the film cost; the writer used this information to prepare a breakdown of the most general sort. While it was commendable of *Life* to explain studio finances in such lucid terms, some of the statements are misleading. *Life* did not have access to a Detail Budget in which music and props would not be listed under "Miscellany" but would have their own budget lines. Of the $85,000 paid for story and script, $50,000 is reported as having gone to Brewer and Bloch for their play. But that sum was a rounding out of the $18,500 that Selznick paid for the rights and the $27,500 that Warners paid Selznick. Here, perhaps, is the source of the error that *Dark Victory* was sold to the movies for $50,000.

Introduction

and totemic awesomeness. The Davis iconography will be complete with her last film; the Davis persona, the screen image of which each role was an emanation, was completed in 1939 with *Dark Victory*. It was approaching its final form in 1938, for there were three earlier films that heightened the tone of her image and deepened the texture: *Marked Woman, That Certain Woman*, and *Jezebel*.

Before *Marked Woman*, it was clear that Davis could suffer or inflict suffering, that she could be upper class or working class. But it had not yet been established that she could be both. Davis needed a role to demonstrate her ability to resolve the polarities and contradictions within a character, a role in which she could radiate a patrician aloofness while espousing proletarian values. In *Marked Woman*, she found such a role. On the surface, Mary Dwight is a "clip-joint hostess" with a breezy indifference to the law. Feeling she is beyond its protection, she misleads a crusading district attorney (Humphrey Bogart) into believing she will help him expose a vice king; instead, she deliberately undermines his credibility by identifying the wrong murderers. But Mary's apathy to organized crime does make her a mercenary whore. She generates a cool but not an arctic self-absorption; it is the selfishness of one who lives by the success scenario, not of one who lives for the self. Basically, she has not abandoned her middle-class values. Her concern for her kid sister is genuine, and although she did not have to tell a customer he would be in trouble with the syndicate when his check bounced, she advised him to leave town and even gave him her address.

When her sister is killed defending her virtue at a party given by mobster Johnny Vanning (Eduardo Ciannelli), Mary can no longer remain neutral. "I'll get you if I have to come back from the grave to do it," she tells Vanning. Her sister's death has changed her from hooker to concerned citizen. When Vanning's thugs disfigure her by slashing her face, she changes again—to crime victim. But the most significant change occurs at the end of the film as Mary and her sisters in the profession disappear in the fog. Mary is dressed in the uniform of the working class—basic proletarian black that levels distinctions and creates anonymity. And her retreat into the night recalls the last shot of *I Am a Fugitive from a Chain Gang* (1932)—the individual returning to the mass and leaving his personality in the evening air.

Marked Woman gave Davis her first opportunity to use her special alchemy to melt the proletarian, the whore, and the martyr into one person. With most stars, toughness and vulnerability are two poses, like panels of a diptych. With Davis, toughness is vulnerability's twin, like a diptych whose panels fold in on themselves rather than open out. The unfolding continued in *That Certain Woman* in which she played another Mary, Mary Donnell, a gangster's widow who became a respectable member of the working class.

Davis's performance in *That Certain Woman* suggested not that she stepped out of one role (moll) and into another (attorney's secretary) but rather that by turning over the one, she discovered the other. Although the film is not one of Davis's favorites, it is significant because it reveals her ability to convey strength without becoming overbearing—something she has rarely been able to do because the scripts catered to her mannerisms or the directors catered to her. In *That Certain Woman*, she was the victim of a tyrannical father-in-law who had her marriage to his son (Henry Fonda) annulled. In the best tradition of the four-handkerchief film, Mary gives up her child, but through choice. Although the character seemed to have too many sides to be believable, Davis found the archetypal source from which the other facets derive: the Mater Dolorosa, or Sorrowing Mother. In her scenes with the child, Davis exhibited a luminous maternity. It may not be possible to imagine Bette Davis turning the act of dressing a baby into an image of domestic poetry, but she did. And few shots flattered her as much as the one in which she looked up from the baby and into the eyes of Henry Fonda. The plot may have been hokey, but there was nothing unreal or artificial about Davis's performance. When she decides to give up her child, there is one telling moment of self-pity when the eyes look stabbed and the lips start to crease, but then quickly tighten in resignation.

That Certain Woman was the first of Davis's four films with Edmund Goulding; the others were *Dark Victory, The Old Maid*

Introduction

(1939), and *The Great Lie* (1941). Other directors may have capitalized on her beauty, but Goulding discovered its wellsprings. One shot in *That Certain Woman* authenticates his discovery and disproves Casey Robinson's claim that he gave Davis her first feminine role—a claim, incidentally, that is at odds with Davis's own belief that Goulding made her look like a movie star for the first time: "I was always a member of the cast—a leading member—but not made special in the way Goulding made me special in this film. And in the last scene . . . I looked *really* like a 'movie star.'"[9] It is the last shot of the film; Davis, dressed in a Victorian tea gown and picture hat and looking somewhat like Garbo but without Garbo's worldweariness, is summoned to the phone to hear the happy ending—the Sorrowing Mother becoming the Blessed Lady.

Next Davis needed a role where self-transcendence led to salvation, a role that would involve sacrifice—not the ultimate sacrifice that would be required in *Dark Victory* but something more than loss of beauty or husband. It must be a sacrifice of the self to redeem the self. As Julie Marsden in *Jezebel*, Davis continued to resolve the paradoxes of Woman, showing that what seemed to be contradictions were petals of the same rose.

Julie Marsden was the precursor of Judith Traherne. Initially, both were self-enraptured women, yet through love each learned humility and resignation—the virtues needed to complete the Davis persona. When Julie asks Pres's forgiveness, she bows to the floor, her gown spreading like a submissive flower:

JULIE: See, Pres, I'm kneeling to you—
PRES: Julie! Don't!
JULIE: I want to, Pres. I must make you forgive me—and love me—as I love you.

But Julie's humility was no more complete than Judith's was when she fell in love with Dr. Steele in *Dark Victory*. To manifest the self one must renounce the self. When Pres (Henry Fonda) contracts yellow fever and is about to be sent to Lazarette Island, Julie begs his wife, Amy (Margaret Lindsay), to let her accom-

9. *Mother Goddam*, p. 95.

Introduction

pany him. At first, Julie's reasons are pragmatic: she understands Creole, Amy doesn't; she is strong, Amy isn't. Finally, Julie must humble herself to her rival: "I ask you humbly for the chance to give proof that I can be brave and strong and unselfish." Judith also needed the opportunity to perform the most selfless of acts: dying alone. She must also humble herself by returning to Steele and admitting her folly: "Forgive me . . . I've been so stupid." When she asks Steele where she can find peace, he replies, "Within yourself."

Julie also found that peace within herself. At the end of *Jezebel*, as she rides in the cart with Pres and the fever victims, she radiates the contentment born of regenerative action. Julie was one of Davis's most paradoxical portraits: a woman humble in her pride and serene in her triumph over the stench of death. Judith Traherne too knew that moment of purity that does not come about by itself. First there is pride, then humility, next the fusion when they are purged of arrogance and self-deprecation; peace follows, and finally victory. But with both Julie and Judith, it was love that made the victory possible.

By 1939, Davis was ready for the ultimate role of a woman who accepts the ultimate reality. The fact that the last film her public would have seen was *The Sisters* did not minimize her achievement in *Jezebel*; by showing her surviving the 1906 San Francisco earthquake, *The Sisters* was the bridge between her triumph over an epidemic (*Jezebel*) and her victory over death (*Dark Victory*). Although not vintage Davis, *The Sisters* saw her coping with a marriage to a failed novelist (Errol Flynn) and managing to avoid the walls collapsing around her during the quake. The end of *The Sisters* also recalled the end of *Marked Woman*; the three sisters (Davis, Anita Louise, Jane Bryan) stand close together as a crane shot captures their solidarity—true sisters from a God's-eye view as opposed to the sisters of the night who pound the pavement at eye level. There are two lines in *The Sisters*—both oxymoronic, both spoken by Errol Flynn—that define the Davis woman in terms of a paradox; a hidden harmony, to use the title of Cavaradossi's first aria in *Tosca*, "Recondita armonia." The lines are: "You have a very exciting se-

Introduction

renity" and "There is a quiet assurance about you, Louise." Unwittingly, Flynn summed it all up.

The Davis persona was now in its final stage, yet there was something sad about its completion. It was rather like a flower in full bloom that would never achieve the same natural perfection. After *Dark Victory*, there were a few new buds (*The Letter, The Great Lie, Now, Voyager*); then the flower metamorphosed into a form of hammered gold. But even when it hardened into cold splendor, the persona was still dazzling.

Auteur and Author

With *Dark Victory*, however, one is speaking of a star at her zenith, not in her descendent. It is almost as if the film were astrally blessed, with Davis getting the right combination of director and screenwriter—a situation she would encounter a few times in the 1940s (*Now, Voyager, Mr. Skeffington, The Corn Is Green*) and once again in 1950 with *All about Eve* when the director and screenwriter were the same person, Joseph L. Mankiewicz.

Davis was fortunate in having Edmund Goulding as her director. In addition to making her look like a movie star in *That Certain Woman*, Goulding, who had written fiction and had coauthored the play *Dancing Mothers* (1924) with Edgar Selwyn, understood how the novel and the drama differed from film. Casey Robinson, whose forte was adaptation, had that understanding too, and later he adapted other works for Davis— Zoë Akins's play *The Old Maid*, Olive Higgins Prouty's novel *Now, Voyager*, Rachel Field's *All This and Heaven Too*, and Emlyn Williams's drama *The Corn Is Green* (with Frank Cavett as coscreenwriter).[10]

As a play, *Dark Victory* was a star vehicle. Goulding realized that in an intimate medium like film, a vehicle could result not so much in a powerful performance as in an overpowering one

10. On Robinson as screenwriter, see Richard Corliss, *Talking Pictures: Screenwriters in the American Cinema, 1927–1973* (Woodstock, N.Y.: Overlook Press, 1974), pp. 284–90.

Introduction

that would leave the audience stunned but unsatisfied. Moviegoers would find it difficult to accept a Judith Traherne who progressed from solipsism to sufferer. Goulding hit upon the idea of giving Judith a confidante, Ann King.[11] There was no such character in the play; the closest Judith had to a friend in the original was the worldly wise novelist Alden Blaine, the type of wisecracking woman immortalized on the stage by Audrey Christie and in films by Eve Arden. But in the movie, Ann is a true friend, the classic second self. Another reason for Goulding's creating Ann is offered by Geraldine Fitzgerald, who played the part:

> The character of Ann was . . . to act as a sort of one-person Greek chorus, so that the central doomed figure would not have to cry for herself. The friend would do it. This was a wonderful idea and strengthened the drama immeasurably (regardless of how it was going to be played or by whom). Edmund Goulding believed that it was the *absence* of such a character in the original . . . that forced Judith into too much suffering and made the play fail. His way, Judith could be brave and debonair, while Ann suffered.[12]

Goulding and Robinson faced another problem: how to humanize Judith without loss of dramatic intensity. Although the screenplay provided the narrative basis for Judith's humanization, it was Davis who carried it out. She must have sensed that Judith would be the touchstone for her other roles. At the time, however, she was so distressed over her divorce from Harmon ("Ham") Nelson that she told Hal Wallis she was too sick to continue filming. "Stay sick" was Wallis's reply. Apparently her affair (or "romance" as she calls it in *The Lonely Life*) with George Brent, who played Steele, made her less despondent; it certainly made Brent less stolid.

For Judith, Davis drew upon every mood she had ever expressed—insouciance, impatience, anger, passion, acquiescence. Judith may have been the opposite of the proletarian

---

11. Although Goulding "contributed greatly" to the screenplay, according to Robinson, one should assume that while Goulding may have had the idea for Ann, Robinson brought that idea to realization.
12. Fitzgerald to Dick, August 19, 1980.

Introduction

woman, yet she could be as restless and flippant as Mary Dwight of *Marked Woman*. But Mary's flippancy was only a veneer for the anger within. Davis used that surface coolness and inner restlessness to define the worldly Judith; for the regenerate Judith, she elaborated on Julie Marsden's outstanding quality—a sense of resignation that was not stoic but beatific.

Davis did more than mine the lode of her interior; she worked at the part. Driving home from the studio at dusk, she would prepare for the moment when Judith goes blind by pretending it was really daylight and trying to look as far into the darkness as she could. Her task was facilitated by Casey Robinson's screenplay, which not only opened up the original but also gave it depth and dimension. A play has its own kind of preliminary action: a prologue, perhaps some precurtain exposition, or a bit of conversation until the incentive moment occurs. But the rhythm of a film cannot be quite so literary. Robinson deferred the opening, where Judith is brought to Steele's office, until he had dramatized the reason for her visit: the accident at the training track when she rode her horse into the jump. Robinson began with Judith in her milieu, F. Scott Fitzgerald's Long Island, where she is surrounded by types that would crash Jay Gatsby's parties but never give any of their own.

Robinson delineated that milieu so successfully that, after the film was released, George Brewer, Jr., revised the play, hoping, no doubt, that stock companies and amateur groups would perform it on the basis of the movie's popularity.[13] Realizing that such organizations had limited means and even more limited budgets, Brewer arranged for Judith to be examined in her Long Island living room, thereby dispensing with the set for Steele's office. But his chief change was the addition of three characters to round out Judith's circle of friends which, originally, comprised only Alden Blaine and her male counterpart, the sybaritic Leslie Clarke. Robinson had a reason for giving Judith a circle of friends; by establishing her dependence on the "kids," as she affectionately calls her cronies, Robinson made her death more

---

13. The revised version is published by Dramatists Play Service.

Introduction

heroic. Judith, who could not bear to live alone, chose to die alone.

Of historical significance is the fact that Alec Hamm, one of the "kids," was played by the fortieth president of the United States, Ronald Reagan. Reagan did not find the film a "rewarding experience," as he states in his autobiography, nor does he regard Alec as one of his favorite roles. Influenced perhaps by the character of Leslie Clarke, Robinson created Alec to offset the conventional masculinity of Steele and provide an interesting contrast to the machismo of horse trainer Michael O'Leary. In the early drafts, Alec was a much larger role, but Robinson gradually reduced it, probably because the character was too superficial to sustain an audience's interest.

Apparently Goulding wanted Reagan to play Alec with an effete, if not an effeminate, airiness (or, as one critic crudely suggested, as if he were Rhonda, not Ronald, Reagan).[14] Reagan claimed that the role was patterned after the director's "earlier life," although he neither identified the director nor explained about that earlier life. Reagan also wanted to play Alec's last scene with Judith "with great sincerity." In the film, however, the scene does not involve Alec. When Judith, in search of a reconciliation, finds Steele at Alec's apartment, Alec exits.

The scene included a line of dialogue that Reagan inflected peculiarly. "You're the one man, so be nice to her," Alec tells Steele. "He [Goulding] didn't get what he wanted, whatever the hell that was, and I ended up not delivering the line the way my instinct told me it should be delivered. It was bad."[15] Reagan delivered the line with the stress on "man," implying that Alec was less than one. That may have been what Goulding intended, but one doubts that audiences got the point. Actually, Reagan played the role well. Looking like one of Fitzgerald's sad young men, he exuded a boozy winsomeness that was neither effete nor effeminate but just mildly decadent.

Robinson's chief problem, however, was with Judith, not her

14. Mitch Tuchman, "Ladies and Gentlemen, the Next President of the United States," *Film Comment*, 16 (July–August 1980), 51.
15. Ronald Reagan with Richard G. Hubler, *Where's the Rest of Me?* (New York: Duell, Sloan and Pearce, 1965), p. 102.

Introduction

circle. Faced with a character whose self-absorption could be as tiresome as her nobility, Robinson worked from the premise that Goulding had set down: Judith must be above self-pity. She may have a moment of despair, but she cannot be a sob sister. She should have a flapper's recklessness but also a self-awareness that the Jazz Daughter lacked. Thus Judith knows her condition is serious: "Confidentially, darling, this is more than a hangover," she confides to Ann. And Davis, who understood paradox as well as any literary critic, delivered the line with fatalistic nonchalance, as if Judith knew the implications of what she had said but was too busy to pursue them.

Robinson made Judith's first encounter with Steele more than the mannered sparring it was in the play. Naturally she must be hostile to him, but there cannot be the battle of the sexes that occurs in romantic comedy. Judith directs her barbs at Steele, who must suffer them until he has to confront her with her condition. But he cannot be smug; Judith is a cancer victim, not an opponent in a contest of wit. It was a difficult scene to write and to act, especially for Davis, since Brent could relax and play it straight. Davis was able to use some of the self-centeredness she gave Mildred in *Of Human Bondage,* softening it until it became a breezy egotism; to it she added the flamboyance of her "blonde period" movies, toning down the theatrics but keeping the theatricality. Moving in a series of arcs and curves, like the helix of smoke from her cigarette, she made her walk into a trajectory as soon as she stepped into Steele's office. She insults him and mocks his profession, doing it brattishly like a child craving attention but too spoiled to work for it. She treats the examination like a game; her eyes closed, she laughs giddily when he administers the touch test. Yet when Steele tells her she must have an operation, Judith lowers her eyes in silent submission.

Inevitably Judith must learn she is dying, but in the meantime the audience must remain interested in her. Although it may seem callous to talk of suspense in the context of a malignancy, Robinson understood that it was precisely the lack of suspense that weakened the play and caused the authors to substitute turgid prose for human drama. This need not have been the case, however. Theoretically, the sooner the audience learns that Judith is doomed, the more anxious it will be for the moment when she learns it as well. Judith discovers the truth not by inferring it from the look in Steele's eyes, as she did in the play, but by coming upon her file on Steele's desk, which is considerably more dramatic.

Once Judith realizes her case is hopeless, she undergoes a radical emotional change. Love turns to hate, hate to despondency, despondency to repentance, repentance to benevolence, the end result being a higher form of love than the kind she felt at the beginning. A playwright might have difficulty dramatizing such transitions, although O'Neill managed them in *Desire under the Elms* (1924) in which hatred yielded to passion, passion to murder, murder to retribution, retribution to redemption. Robinson portrayed Judith's transformation in much the same way—as a process, not a sudden metamorphosis. First she returns to her old ways, reveling in the dissipation that comes from self-destructiveness. Without Steele, Judith would probably have destroyed herself if the tumor had not done so. Since she has a child's candor, she rails at him for being dishonest. Eventually Judith goes back to Steele, but her motives gave Robinson some difficulty.

In the play, it was the shock of recognition after a romantic interlude with Michael that sent her back to Steele, although her decision was too sudden to be anything more than a second act curtain line. In the film, the scene between Michael (Humphrey Bogart) and Judith, now set in the stables, is a model of screenwriting. Robinson labored over it, as the drafts show, for it was the kind of scene that lent itself to dark rhetoric; the dialogue would also sound like bad graveyard poetry if Robinson pursued the implications of a dying woman's telling a healthy male that he has just tried to seduce a corpse, as Judith does in the play. Originally, when Judith told Michael she was going to die, he cried: "Don't you know, you can be damned to Hell for sayin' less than that?" Judith's reply was in the best tradition of the drawing room rejoinder: "I can't—I've been there." Yet Robinson thought of retaining that line. In retrospect, it would have been the worst kind of Bette Davis line—the melodramatic clincher that her mimics adore and that, unfortunately, has become synonymous with her name. Robinson finally discarded it; the purpose of the scene was not to reveal Judith's flair for melodrama but to disclose a dimension of her personality that had not been previously seen—her sexuality.

Although Judith is not promiscuous, she has had lovers and is often "on the town," as one young man puts it. But death will rob her of her sexuality. Thus when she is in the stables with Michael, she is deliberately seductive, as if she were trying to see if she can still be attractive to men. She plays the aristocrat to his commoner, Constance Chatterley to his Mellors. Michael is a Lawrentian male who deifies his manhood. Judith has always been fascinated by him although she has never treated him as an equal. In a scene of class-conscious eroticism, she slowly lights a cigarette, throwing the match on the stable floor. "What are you trying to do? Burn us up?" he asks. Judith's reply is powerfully ambivalent: "Are you afraid to burn, Michael? Are you afraid to die?" She is speaking in erotic code that is too complex for him. It was a double question, implying that burning and death, Eros and Thanatos, were related. Since Michael does not understand the connection, he replies only to the second part: "I wouldn't want to die while you're alive, Miss Judith."

When Michael tries to make love to her, Judith is forced to admit she is dying. Michael's new response is: "Heaven forgive you for sayin' a thing like that!" Judith's reply is not so much to Michael's outburst as to what it implies: "Heaven forgive me. When it comes, it must be met beautifully and finely." Now the scene has the motivation it needs. Judith experiences more than just a pang of conscience; she has a true revelation as she associates Michael's exclamation with the words Steele had spoken to her earlier. The combined associations of heaven's forgiveness and death met beautifully send her back to Steele.

Robinson shot the stables scene himself since Goulding did not think it should be in the movie and refused to film it. It is an impressive scene, both for the tautness of the writing and the smoldering eroticism that burns out into repentance. It was Davis, however, not Bogart, who dominated the scene. Physically, Bogart had the right kind of sullen masculinity for Michael, but it smelled of the street, not the stables, and the Irish accent only made the character seem quaint. Throughout the scene, Davis seemed to be trying to find the source of Bogart's sexual energy so she could connect with it, only to discover that it was flowing into the camera and not into her. Mary Astor would have better luck finding it in *The Maltese Falcon* (1941), and Lauren Bacall would patent the source in *To Have and Have Not* (1944) and *The Big Sleep* (1946).

Luckily, Robinson did not defer to Goulding; otherwise Judith's return to Steele would have been nothing but a sudden conversion. Now she can accept death because she has revealed a moral center beneath the frivolous façade. But her decision cannot reek of piety. Just as Mary Donnell never made a noble gesture out of giving up her child in *That Certain Woman*, Judith does not turn death into a platonic form or into something ontologically beautiful. She dies with dignity, but dignity is a human attribute, not an aesthetic consideration. As Judith packs Steele off to New York, where presumably he will win recognition for his research, she says, "And with each blow you strike you can say, 'That was for Judith, my wife,'" pricking the line with a jab of anger as if the old Judith were lashing out at her new self.

Robinson found the mean between the noble and the aesthetic. There is nothing noble about death, nor is it dignified in itself. One must impart dignity to it. Robinson therefore refrains from poeticizing Judith's death and instead dramatizes the symptoms indicating that the end is near. The first comes with a chilling naturalness: Judith casually observes that the sun has gone down but then feels its rays on her hands. Next there are the farewells—not operatic addios but acts of simple finality: packing her husband's suitcase, planting the hyacinths, dismissing Ann, embracing the dogs, and kneeling in prayer. These actions, unmarred by show or sentiment, gave Judith's death its dignity.

From the very beginning, Robinson and Goulding agreed that *Dark Victory* would not end with Judith's death; it would be the penultimate scene, as the treatment and early drafts attest. To

Introduction

anticipate the ending, which would be set at the Grand National, Judith, before her death, would instruct Ann about the way her box should be decorated and who should be invited to the reception. Of course, there was no need to show the Grand National since it was hardly integral to the plot. Yet Robinson and Goulding felt the scene would be an emotional palliative and would confirm what had already been suggested—the union of Steele and Ann.

The scene was shot, and the film ended with Steele and Ann facing each other as the camera craned up to the treetops. The *Variety* reviewer (March 7, 1939), who saw the original version, criticized the final scene, which lasted about five minutes, claiming that it was anticlimactic. Warners agreed, and it was cut; Geraldine Fitzgerald also thought that it "reduced the cathartic effect" of the tragedy. Anything would have been anticlimactic after the close-up of Judith's face as it went out of focus, although one suspects that the shot was originally meant to be a slow dissolve to Belmont Race Track.

Robinson's contribution to *Dark Victory* can be seen by comparing the film with the play and preliminary drafts of the screenplay; Goulding's contribution, however, is less obvious. His touches were subtle, so much so that they often went unnoticed.[16] For example, Goulding avoided having his characters walk out of frame, preferring that they exit through a door as they would on stage. Thus, after a conversation with Ann, Judith walks out of Ann's room and into the hall where she stops and talks with the maid. This is true *mise-en-scène:* the staging of an action so that it acquires lifelikeness. Another example of Goulding's subtlety is his treatment of Ann as surrogate sufferer. Robinson went along with this idea, even taking a line from the play that Judith speaks—a line tinged with cynicism—and reassigning it to Ann. In the play, when Steele informs Judith that death will come peacefully, she replies,

16. Little seems to have been written on Goulding except for Richard Koszarski's introduction to Goulding's essay, "The Talkers in Close-Up," in *Hollywood Directors: 1914–1940* (New York: Oxford University Press, 1976), p. 205; and William R. Meyer, *Warner Brothers Directors: The Hard-Boiled, the Comic, and the Weepers* (New Rochelle: N.Y.: Arlington House, 1978), pp. 143–53.

Introduction

"God's last small mercy." In the film, Ann speaks the line. She can afford to be sardonic; Judith cannot. Similarly, Judith gets Alden Blaine's flip remark that America should have been colonized by the Spanish or French instead of the Puritans.

Dialogue alone does not suggest that one character is another's alter ego. Goulding had to make the point visually, as he did in several shots, notably one in which Ann is seated behind Judith in the hospital room, smoking a cigarette as Judith might. If Ann must suffer, she must also assume the suffering pose as she frequently does, cupping her cheek in her hand or pressing her hand against her face.

Because it was intimated that Steele and Ann would marry after Judith's death, Goulding adumbrated their union with frequent two-shots. The casting also enabled the audience to think of Ann and Steele as a potential couple. Physically, Brent and Fitzgerald were suited to each other; they even had the same coloring. In *Mildred Pierce* (1945), Michael Curtiz also tried to deepen the narrative by emphasizing resemblances among the three main characters. When Joan Crawford, Zachary Scott, and Ann Blyth appear in the same shot, one notices that they all not only have dark hair but also have the same flesh tones and wear the same noirish clothes.

If Goulding favored a particular composition, it was the three-shot, which he often used as a prefiguring device, reserving it for occasions when one of the characters would be affected by a forthcoming event. In *That Certain Woman*, when Mary's father-in-law demands that the marriage be annulled, Goulding frames the shot with father and son in profile and Mary in the background. In *The Dawn Patrol* (1938), when Errol Flynn tells a young flier he will be in the air the next morning, David Niven stands aghast in the background.

In *Dark Victory*, Goulding added overtones of interwoven destinies to the three-shot. Before her surgery, Judith is in a hospital bed, center of frame, with Steele left and Ann right. As soon as she expresses her wish that Steele and Ann be friends, Goulding cuts to a two-shot of Steele and Ann, which implies that eventually they will be more than friends. When Judith comes out on the terrace immediately after Steele has told Ann

Introduction

she is going to die, Goulding groups the three of them together: Judith, back to camera, facing Steele on the left and Ann on the right. Later, when Judith, virtually blind, asks Ann to read the letter summoning Steele to New York, she is in the center of the frame, with Steele on the left and Ann on the right.

Like every true film maker, Goulding knew when images were more potent than words. Although Robinson was an accomplished screenwriter, his visual sense could often go awry. In the final script, he had one of the dogs in the death scene lying on the floor of Judith's bedroom with its head on its paws. Fortunately, the dog—or, rather, the two dogs—stay downstairs in the film, nor does Judith utter the saintly line, "Oh, yes, Martha," when her housekeeper inquires if she is all right—a strange question to ask the dying.

Goulding simply has Judith ease herself onto the bed as the camera tracks up to her face, which gradually goes out of focus. There are many ways of representing death in film: a body silhouetted against a wall, a rocking chair lashed by the rain, a bathrobe caught in the tide. But each is precisely that—a representation, a reduction of the person to an image or an object. Goulding reduces death to a naked metaphor, a universal image: the loss of focus and the termination of vision.

Music

As a composer (his best known song is "Mam'selle" from *The Razor's Edge*, 1946), Goulding knew that music can be an effective bridge between scenes. It was not enough just to use wipes to keep the narrative fluid; wipes are excellent scene-changers but they do not produce unity. Although Goulding relies on the wipe as a transitional device, he uses music as a bridge. In fact, it is music that connects three successive scenes so that they form a sequence: Judith's discovering the truth about her condition, her bitter reaction to Steele and Ann at the restaurant, and her despondency in the bar. The impact of "Prognosis Negative" sends her rushing out of Steele's office as the Blindness theme surges from the soundtrack. Suddenly there is a wipe to a fashionable restaurant where an orchestra is playing a Strauss waltz

Introduction

whose gaiety is in marked contrast to the music of the previous scene. Unable to observe the amenities, Judith exits to the accompaniment of violins. Again there is an abrupt change of music and setting. The sedate orchestra yields to a combo as another wipe transfers the action to a bar where a drunken Judith pays the band fifty dollars for a reprise of "Oh! Give Me Time for Tenderness" (which Goulding composed to lyrics by Elsie Janis).

Although the "Oh! Give Me Time for Tenderness" scene is undeniably moving, when one speaks of the music in *Dark Victory*, one means Max Steiner's score, which is built on three themes: Blindness (Judith's theme), Resignation, and Winter.[17] The Blindness theme pervades the film; it is a stark phrase composed for vibraphone, piano, celesta, and harp.[18]

In its simplest form, Blindness denoted fate at its most inexorable. With a change of tempo, it became less threatening, but never lush or romantic enough to dispel the aura of inevitability that it evoked. Resignation is scored for strings; it is generally dignified except for a lapse into Old South teariness. One wonders if Steiner had a few chords left over from *Jezebel*. Although Resignation cannot compare with Blindness in complexity (nor, for that matter, can Winter, which has a familiar but unmemorable bounciness), it was the music heard during the opening credits. Certainly Resignation made a better prelude than Blindness, which would have been too somber, especially after the ceremonious two-bar phrase (which Steiner also composed) that always accompanied the WB shield.

Blindness was a true leitmotif; it was as if it had a mind of its own, knowing when and how to appear: softly, just before surgery, when Judith pitifully asked Steele to find some sense in the head he would be opening up; hauntingly, when Dr. Par-

---

17. The music for *Dark Victory* can be heard in *Classic Film Scores for Bette Davis* (RCA Victor, ARL 1–0183; 1973).

18. I am grateful to Dr. James Pegolotti, Dean of Arts and Sciences, Western Connecticut State College, for transcribing the Blindness theme so it could be reproduced here.

sons looked in on Judith after the operation, sadly remarking that he brought her into the world; eerily, when Judith proposed to Steele, unaware that the surgery was unsuccessful; and in hurried waltztime, as if the notes knew they could not tarry, when Judith gave Steele a pair of gold cuff links in gratitude for "saving" her life.

Although Resignation was musically inferior to Blindness, it had a sentimental power that suited the scene in which Judith explained to Steele that their marriage was a victory over the dark. Once Steiner combined Blindness and Resignation: Judith begged Steele's forgiveness to the Resignation music that then flowed into Blindness without a break. Inevitably *Dark Victory* would end with Blindness, this time played with a soothing otherworldliness as Judith's face goes out of focus—the music working in conjunction with the camera to make the same narrative point.

The Significance of *Dark Victory*

As Film of Terminal Illness

Dark Victory was not the first movie with a fatally ill heroine. Several *Camilles* preceded it; *One Way Passage* (1932) starred Kay Francis as a socialite suffering from heart disease; *Three Comrades* (1938) featured Margaret Sullavan as a consumptive. Although ladies with delicate hearts and tubercular heroines were not unfamiliar to moviegoers, a woman with a malignancy was. *Dark Victory* not only portrayed such a character but also depicted terminal illness with a detail that was previously unknown.

To insure "scrupulous precision of the medical details,"[19] Casey Robinson and David Lewis consulted specialists at the Cedars of Lebanon Hospital in Los Angeles. But Brewer and Bloch had also done their homework. The neurological examination that Steele administers to Judith in the film existed in the original. Robinson drew on the symptoms described in the play. He also added a scene in which Judith collapsed on the stairs and another in which she told Ann about colliding with a woman on the street. In both the play and the film, Steele be-

---

19. Charles Higham, *Warner Brothers* (New York: Scribner's, 1975), p. 137.

Introduction

came interested in Judith's case when he learned that she steered her horse into the *right* wing of the jump and burned her *right* hand while smoking. The tumor was obviously in the left hemisphere of the brain, a fact that explained the loss of sensation in her right hand and her inability to tell whether a substance was soft or hard, fine or coarse when she touched it with her right hand.[20]

In addition to being medically accurate, *Dark Victory* anticipated, with interesting variations, the five responses of the terminally ill that Elisabeth Kübler-Ross identified in *On Death and Dying* (1969): denial and isolation, anger, bargaining, depression, acceptance.[21] It is incorrect, however, to assume that Judith is the one who goes through each stage. If she did, she would merely be a case history and the film the record of a cancer patient. Judith does not deny the truth, but her alter ego, Ann, does: "Oh, don't listen to him," Ann cries when Steele

---

20. In the opinion of three specialists, the medical details are authentic. Leonard I. Malis, M.D., professor and chairman of the Department of Neurosurgery at Mount Sinai School of Medicine, agrees that "*Dark Victory* has a reasonable basis in neurosurgical fact for the symptom presentation and development." His only objection—and it is a professional, not an artistic one—is that, given her type of tumor, Judith would probably have experienced progressive aphasia and mental deterioration before blindness. On the other hand, Dr. Malis admits that "the development of such symptoms would . . . not be compatible with the plot of the story and to this extent the rare but possible absence of these more common symptoms can probably be excused" (Malis to Dick, September 17, 1980). Thomas J. Fahey, M.D., director of Outpatient Services at Memorial Sloan-Kettering Cancer Center, terms the examination "a reasonable facsimile" and notes that the dimming of vision or amblyopia that Judith experiences would be consistent with a tumor in the left hemisphere of the brain: "All in all, it seems the authors . . . had some type of neurological consultation" (Fahey to Dick, September 16, 1980). To J. Scott Martin, director of the Department of Neurosurgery at Geisinger Medical Center, the film presents "a reasonable description of the patient with a glioma allowing for some artistic license." Apropos of Judith's inability to remember if she saw a play in the afternoon and played bridge in the evening or vice versa, Dr. Martin observes that "decreased mental capacity and memory loss for recent events are common. Patients can remember their high school teacher but not what they had for breakfast" (Martin to Dick, September 3, 1980).

21. Rita TheBerge seems to have been the first to see a connection between *Dark Victory* and Kübler-Ross's five stages; see *Cinema Texas Program Notes*, 17 (September 27, 1979), 70–73.

Introduction

insists on surgery. When Steele tells Ann that Judith will die, her response is a mixture of denial and anger: "No, that isn't true. You shouldn't have touched her." When Judith becomes angry, she directs her anger not at fate or God but at Steele for deceiving her. Steele is the one who laments the absence of a cure for "a girl like that—so alive—so entitled to live." Judith bargains, not to buy time so she can live longer but so she can die without her husband's being present—hence, the hurried send-off to New York. Judith falls into depression, but it is brief. She considers suicide: "Would I be wrong if I made it happen?" she asks Ann, whose shocked reaction terminates the discussion. When Steele thinks of taking his life, Judith dissuades him ("You couldn't be that unkind to me") as Ann had dissuaded her. With the creation of Ann as alter ego and the intimation that Steele would be her future husband, the five reactions could be divided among the three principals, and Judith could be kept from slipping into solitary anguish.

Since medical and thanatological accuracy does not make a film a classic, *Dark Victory* was unusual because the script blended romance and drama in the right proportions. The result was true popular tragedy. *Dark Victory* popularized the conventions of tragedy, offering not a department store heroine or a struggling housewife but an heiress whose social status would be the equivalent of the tragic protagonist's royal stock. The heroine treads the classic path of reversal and recognition as she progresses from ignorance to self-knowledge. Under the circumstances, a tragic flaw would have been excessive; a flawed body was enough.

For various reasons, most films about terminal illness never achieve the distinction of popular tragedy. Some stress romance at the expense of tragedy and become maudlin—for example, *'Til We Meet Again* (1940), the remake of *One Way Passage; Sentimental Journey* (1946) and its remake, *The Gift of Love* (1958); others stress tragedy at the expense of romance and become lugubrious—*Bobby Deerfield* (1977), the TV movie *A Private Battle* (1980), which dramatized Cornelius Ryan's death from cancer. Then there are those that use terminal illness as a means of getting rid of a character. Kay Miniver's cancer in *The Miniver*

Introduction

Story (1950), the sequel to *Mrs. Miniver* (1942), was a convenient way of killing off a woman whose wartime courage would have no place in peacetime England and whose death would preclude the possibility of further films about her.

A film can even include the staples and still not measure up to the original. *The Other Love* (1947), produced by David Lewis and based on Erich Maria Remarque's "Beyond," resembled *Dark Victory* in regard to Karen Duncan, the doomed heroine (Barbara Stanwyck), her doctor-lover (David Niven), and her fling before repentance—this time in Monte Carlo with a gambler (Richard Conte). But Karen's disease (consumption) was cinematically safe, and her profession (concert pianist) gave her an aura that even an heiress would lack.

Stolen Hours (1963), the remake of *Dark Victory*, had even more of the staples; in fact, it repeated most of the original's plot devices and character types: the heiress, the doctor she marries, the discovery of the file, the spree before marriage, the village to which the couple retire (this time in Cornwall, since the remake was set in England), and the solitary death. One character was conspicuously absent: Ann. Her closest equivalent would be the heroine's sister. But a sister is not the same as a friend. Consequently, there was no sharing of suffering and no real bond between the sister and the heroine's husband. As often happens with remakes, gloss replaced sincerity. Today one thinks of *Stolen Hours*, if one thinks of it at all, as tragically prophetic: Susan Hayward, who played the heroine (now called Laura Pember), died of a brain tumor herself in 1975.

Two films, made shortly before the end of Hollywood's Golden Age, aspired to the level of *Dark Victory*: one of them, *No Sad Songs for Me* (1950), attempted a similar blend of romance and tragedy; the other, *An Act of Murder* (1948), substituted a moral issue for romance.

There were obvious differences between *Dark Victory* and *No Sad Songs for Me* in which Margaret Sullavan played the role of Mary Scott, a terminally ill wife and mother. Since Mary was never a high-living socialite, she did not undergo a transformation. Yet, like Judith, Mary realized her husband would need someone to replace her. Thus the plot included an "Ann

Introduction

figure," Chris Radna (Viveca Lindfors). Although Mary's actual death is never shown on the screen, the film ends affirming the sentiments expressed in the title. Chris and Mary's young daughter are at the piano, playing an arrangement of the last movement of Brahms's First Symphony, which has a stateliness about it that never expands into pomposity. Musically, it is the quintessence of death with dignity, although there is no visual correlative as there was at the end of *Dark Victory*.

On the other hand, a romantic approach would not have suited *An Act of Murder* because Catherine Cooke (Florence Eldridge), who was dying of a brain tumor, was middle-aged. In its place, the script substituted mercy killing. Except for the didacticism at the end, the film is extraordinarily powerful. In one scene, Catherine suffers such pain that she smashes a perfume bottle against a mirror, leaving it a spider's web of shattered glass. At an amusement park, her head begins to throb in a hall of mirrors as her agony is reproduced in a myriad of reflections.[22]

As the public has grown more cancer-conscious, terminal illness has become a recurrent theme in movies made for television. Even *Dark Victory* was seen there in 1976 in an overlong version with Elizabeth Montgomery and Anthony Hopkins; the script reflected the changing times by giving Judith a career—television producer. Often they were biographical: *Brian's Song* (1970), the story of Chicago Bears football player Brian Piccolo; *Babe* (1975), a dramatization of the life of Babe Didrikson Zaharias; *Death Be Not Proud* (1975), John Gunther's account of his son's death from a brain tumor; and the previously mentioned *A Private Battle*. A few (*Brian's Song, Babe*) were genuinely affecting, but most of them were either more concerned with

---

22. Other films about terminal illness include *The Hasty Heart* (1949), in which the protagonist is a Scottish soldier dying of kidney disease; *Cleo from 5 to 7* (1962), *Love Story* (1970), *Love and Pain (and the Whole Damn Thing)* (1972), *Bang the Drum Slowly* (1973), *No Time for Breakfast* (1975), *Promises in the Dark* (1979), and *Tribute* (1980). In addition to the TV movies mentioned below there is *The Shadow Box* (1980), Michael Cristofer's adaptation of his 1977 Pulitzer Prize play, which is an improvement over the original, notably in its omission of the self-consciously poetic coda.

Introduction

dying than with death or used cancer as a plot device—as a means of reconciling mother and daughter (*Strangers: The Story of a Mother and Daughter*, 1979) or father and son (*Homeward Bound*, 1980). *Dark Victory*, on the other hand, connected death and dying as theory and practice, preparation and execution.

As Woman's Film

Dark Victory is invariably called a woman's film, a term that is difficult to define because it seems so self-evident. Molly Haskell, who devotes an entire chapter to the woman's film in *From Reverence to Rape*, simply calls it one in which "the woman—a woman—is at the center of the universe."[23] Although some consider the woman's film a genre, it seems too limited in subject matter and too deficient in conventions to warrant that designation. Film romance would be the genre; the woman's film, a species or type of romance. If one thinks of the woman's film as a type rather than a form, one may be more sympathetic to a film that transcends its type. One expects more of a genre because it has a broader appeal and a greater potential for art. Therefore, when a woman's film achieves both universality and excellence, it is because the woman at the center is a special kind of woman—woman at her best, woman learning the meaning of mortality and thus gaining the highest form of tragic knowledge. When a film reaches this level, the woman becomes someone whose concerns extend beyond her sex to humankind.

If *Dark Victory* is a woman's film, it should follow the woman's film formula in which the heroine is a victim—of a jealous lover (any version of *Smilin' Through*), of a jealous rival (*In Name Only*, 1939), of a tragic marriage (*A Woman of Affairs*, 1929), of an insensitive parent (*The Barretts of Wimpole Street*, 1934), of a vindictive mother-in-law (any version of *Madame X*), of a vindictive father-in-law (*That Certain Woman*). Sometimes she is victimized by hard times (either version of *Waterloo Bridge*), mother love (either *Stella Dallas*), a child's selfishness (*Mildred Pierce*) or her own (*Mr. Skeffington*, 1944). If the plot does not consign her

23. Molly Haskell, *From Reverence to Rape: The Treatment of Women in the Movies* (New York: Holt, Rinehart and Winston, 1974), p. 155.

Introduction

to a state of tragic isolation, she may have a kindly housekeeper or nanny (*The Barretts of Wimpole Street*), a pragmatic sidekick (*Waterloo Bridge*), or a confidante who is more of a good listener than a friend (*Mildred Pierce*). As a mother, she may be called upon to make further sacrifices—giving up her child (*White Banners*, 1938; *The Old Maid*, 1939) or having her child taken from her (*Madame X*). Occasionally she encounters her child in the most unlikely places—in a courtroom where the lawyer-son finds himself defending his own mother (*Madame X*); in London during the Blitz (*To Each His Own*, 1946). If she ever finds love, it is often the redemptive kind that the virtuous offers the transgressor (*The Shopworn Angel*, 1938). But whether she is wife, mother, or mistress, she must suffer.

Dark Victory clearly was not a formula film. Judith is a victim of cancer, and nothing else. Goulding and Robinson saw to it that she did not monopolize her suffering. Although Ann is her employee, the two women have a far deeper relationship than do Ida and Mildred Pierce. Since Judith's condition rules out children, her tragedy is not obscured by maternity that is frustrated or denied. While Steele's love is redemptive, her ability to return it gives meaning to his life as well. Finally, *Dark Victory* is a woman's film primarily because a woman is at the center; it is a classic because we are all at the center, sharing a woman's confrontation with her mortality as if it were our own. By portraying a human being facing the ultimate—and universal—reality, *Dark Victory* brought the woman's film to its apogee. Nothing lay beyond it, for there is nothing beyond death met finely. Death met finely is transfiguration.

Therefore, the cycle began anew. The woman's films Davis made after *Dark Victory* were formulaic, especially in terms of the child motif. Davis became an actual or a surrogate mother. In *The Old Maid* she gave up her child; in *The Great Lie* she struggled to keep the friend's child she had raised as her own. *Now, Voyager* (1942) saw her as a surrogate mother to her lover's daughter, and *Old Acquaintance* (1943) as a surrogate mother to her friend's daughter. As Miss Moffat in *The Corn Is Green* (1945) she adopted the illegitimate child of her star pupil whom she sent from the Welsh coal mines to Oxford.

Introduction

Since these movies were more representative of the woman's film than is *Dark Victory*, one can understand their appeal, especially during World War II when women comprised such a large segment of the moviegoing public. Even more understandable is the appeal of the 1940s' woman's film depicting women in actual combat (*Cry Havoc*, 1943; *So Proudly We Hail*, 1943) or waiting anxiously at home (*Tender Comrade*, 1943; *Since You Went Away*, 1944). *Dark Victory*, however, was not rooted in any particular time or place. It had nothing to do with women at war or women who had been exploited. It was made at a time when death could still be portrayed within a context that had no historical associations as opposed to the patriotic woman's film that was set against a background of global war.

Dark Victory is timeless, for it is about facing death itself, not death in battle or in any other setting that would evoke a particular response from the audience—a response that might not be repeated in another era. Finally, Judith's concerns have nothing in common with those of the victimized heroine. One doubts that meeting death finely would have any meaning to Stella Dallas or Mildred Pierce.

If there is an art of living, there is also one of dying. Except for *Dark Victory*, no woman's film has ever shown how that art can be mastered because no woman's film—and few films of any type—have ever had a protagonist like Judith Traherne who was willing to master that art.

1. *Ann as surrogate sufferer.*

2. *A Goulding three-shot (Judith unites her two "friends").*

3. *Another Goulding three-shot, with Judith's back to camera, intimating that the friends will become a couple.*

4. *Judith and the sad young man.*

The Davis Persona: Her Infinite Variety

5. *Seductive ("Are you afraid to burn, Michael?").*

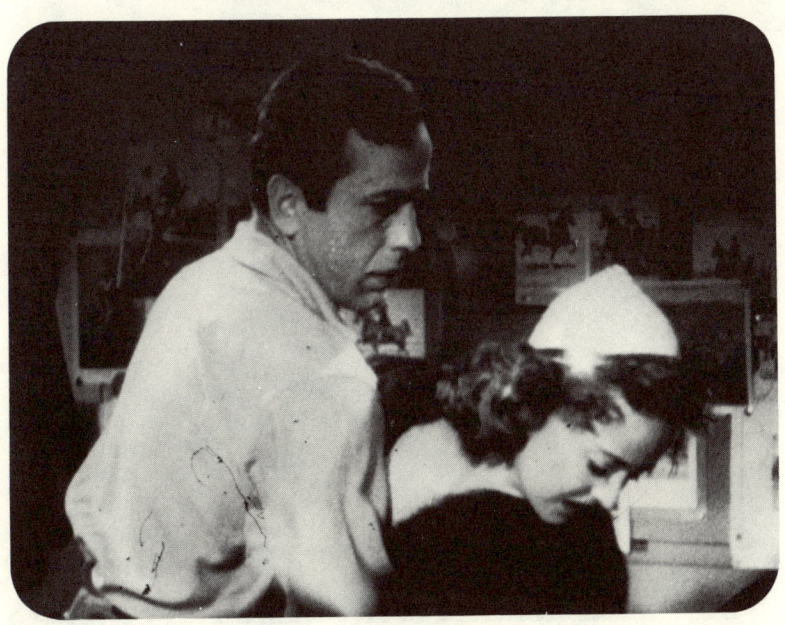

6. *Repentant ("I just can't die like this").*

7. Despondent (Judith at the bar, meditating on the lyrics of "Oh! Give Me Time for Tenderness").

8. Resisting ("Suppose we just don't talk about it").

9. *Imperious (Judith in a hospital bed).*

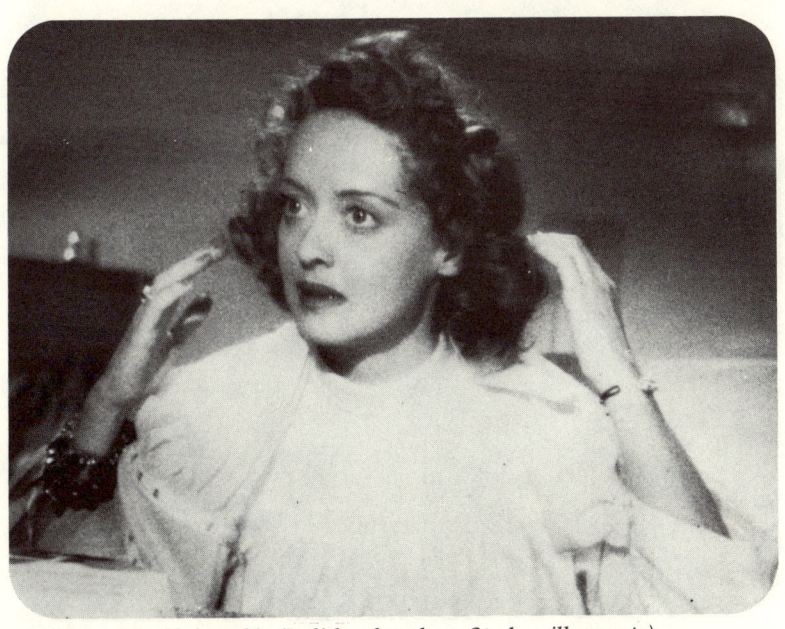
10. *Vulnerable (Judith asks where Steele will operate).*

The Death of Judith

11. *Recognition.*

12. *Packing the suitcase.*

13. *Planting the hyacinths.*

14. *Dismissing Ann.*

15. *Farewell to the dogs.*

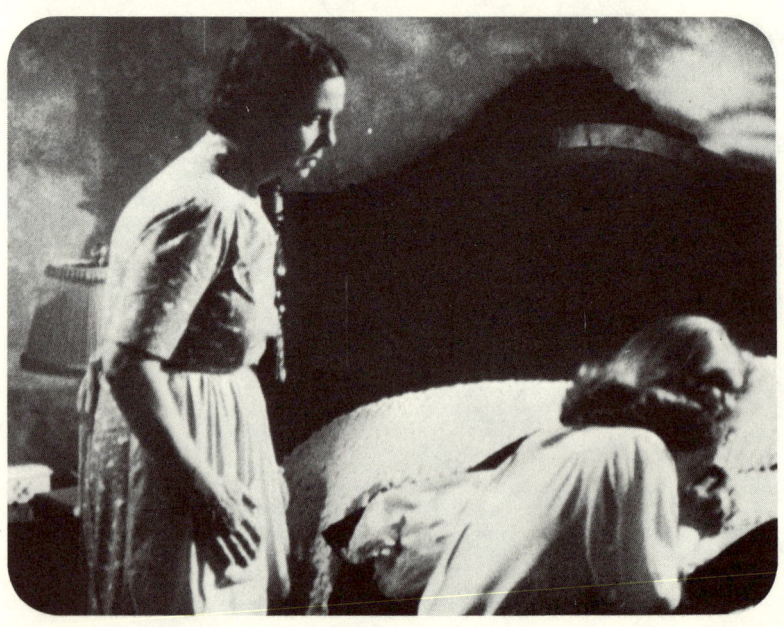
16. *The last prayer.*

17. *Resignation.*

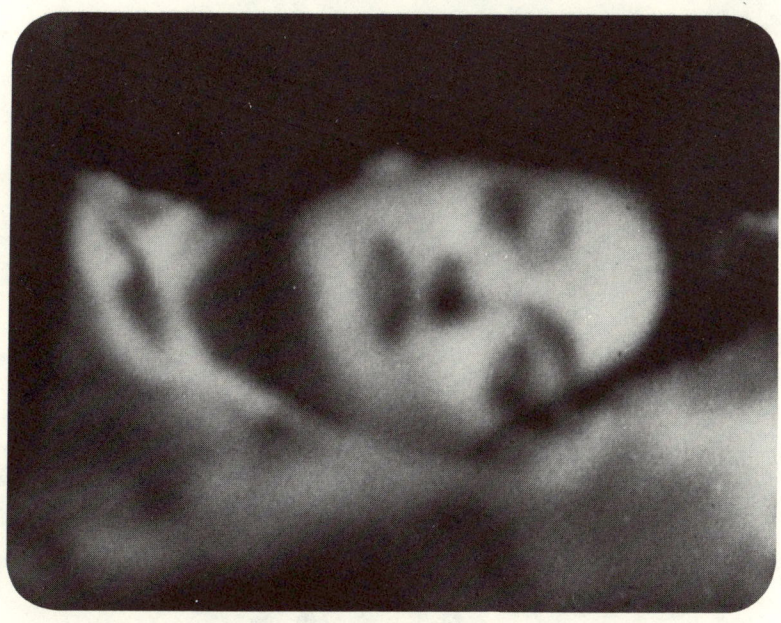
18. *The ultimate fade out.*

Dark Victory

Screenplay
by
CASEY ROBINSON
From the play by
GEORGE BREWER, JR.
and
BERTRAM BLOCH

Dark Victory

    FADE IN
1.   INT. JUDITH'S KITCHEN (EARLY MORNING)   DAY
    CLOSE SHOT   TELEPHONE
ringing. (It has been ringing insistently for some time. We have heard it throughout most of the credit titles.)[1]

2.   PAN SHOT   LUCY
comes to phone. It is clear she has been awakened by the sound of its ringing. She is very, very sleepy—disgruntled. She is in her nightclothes.

LUCY (into phone):
    Miss Traherne's residence . . . (Pause.) Do you realize it's five-thirty in the morning?[2]

Agatha appears behind her, hugging her bathrobe around her neck.

AGATHA (annoyed):
    Who *is* it, Lucy?

LUCY:
    That Michael! (Into phone.) There was a party here last night and the last guest hasn't driven out of the driveway yet . . . Hold on . . .

During the last part of the above, the house phone buzzer has been sounding incessantly. Lucy manipulates the buttons on the control box so as to take the house call.

LUCY:
    Kitchen . . . Lucy speaking . . .

3. INT. ANN'S ROOM   CLOSE SHOT   ANN
is sitting on the edge of the bed, speaking into the telephone. She wears sleeping pajamas.

ANN:
> Lucy, what's the racket? The phone's been ringing all over the house. (Pause.) I'll talk to him. (Manipulates control box buttons, speaks to Michael.) Michael, what do you mean at this unholy hour . . .

4. INT. FEED ROOM   CLOSE SHOT   MICHAEL AT PHONE
In an easy attitude, he is seated in a saddle on a crossbar. He is puffing on his pipe as he talks. Evidently he has been up for hours and is bright and cheerful.

MICHAEL:
> Good morning, Miss Ann. It's a cheerful day now, isn't it? I was wondering if I might speak to Miss Judith.

5. ANN

ANN:
> You certainly might not. She hasn't had two hours' sleep. I wouldn't disturb her for the world.

6. INT. JUDITH'S BEDROOM   CLOSE SHOT   JUDITH
in bed rolls over sleepily and picks up the phone beside her bed.[3]

JUDITH:
> This is Miss Judith Traherne of the sleepy Trahernes.

7. MICHAEL

MICHAEL:
> Is it now? Well, this is Mr. Michael O'Leary of the wide-awake O'Learys. We've got a customer for

that colt. We can get ten thousand if we snatch it quick.

8. JUDITH

JUDITH:
If you mean Challenger, not ten and not twenty. My head's just woozy—not vacant.

9. MICHAEL

MICHAEL (who is enjoying this little clash):
If you don't mind my saying so, Miss Traherne, it might be a good idea for you to take charge of the cups and ribbons and leave the handling of the horses to me.

10. JUDITH

JUDITH (she becomes angry, crisp and businesslike; into phone):
I do mind your saying so. You had your orders last night.

11. WIDER ANGLE   JUDITH AND ANN
Judith hangs up the phone as Ann comes in through the dressing room.

JUDITH:
I ought to slap that man's face.

ANN (opening curtains):
Michael's impertinent sometimes, but he's just about the best trainer money can buy.

Martha, followed by Terry, comes in through the corridor door.[4] The maid, too, has just awakened and is not yet dressed.

MARTHA:
I had the most awful nightmare. I dreamed the phone was ringing all night.

Dark Victory

She comes to help Judith on with her robe.

JUDITH:
For once dreams came true.

ANN:
Bring some coffee, Martha.

MARTHA:
Right away. (She goes out.)

JUDITH (to Terry):
Hi, pal. (Gets out of bed. An attack of dizziness makes her sit back on the bed. Laughing.) Whee! I want to ride on the merry-go-round! (Pushes playful dog.) Go 'way, Terry!

12. ANN
as she seriously scrutinizes her.

JUDITH'S VOICE (laughing):
I'm absolutely giddy . . . I really am!

13. WIDER ANGLE   THE TWO
as Ann comes to her.

ANN:
Another headache, darling?

JUDITH (laughs):
Um! A hangover you could hang your hat on.

She reaches up her hands. Ann helps her to her feet.

ANN:
From what? You didn't touch a drop last night.

JUDITH:
I did so. Gallons. (Walks toward dressing room, weaving a bit, laughing.) Look at me . . . I couldn't pass a sobriety test if the line was a block wide.

ANN (following her):
I watched you. As fast as you were handed

Dark Victory

cocktails, you slipped them into the flower bowls. It was your petunias that got tight, not you.

14. INT. JUDITH'S DRESSING ROOM   JUDITH AND ANN come in during Ann's speech above.
The room is a combination dressing room and bathroom situated between Ann's room and Judith's suite of sitting room and bedroom.
Judith goes to the washbowl, reaches for the water tap, misses it, wobbles.

JUDITH (laughs):
You're silly if you don't believe me.

ANN (scrutinizing her):
I'm going to send for Dr. Parsons.

15. CLOSE-UP   JUDITH
as she registers a strong reaction.

JUDITH (sharply):
No!

16. WIDER ANGLE   BOTH
Ann is astonished at Judith's vehemence. Judith realizes she has made a slip and covers up by preparing to brush her teeth.

JUDITH:
I'll be all right in a minute. If you must be helpful, mix me one of those horrible fruit salts things.

She starts to brush her teeth. She is purposely industrious about it. Ann continues to scrutinize her for a moment, then goes to the medicine cabinet and starts to mix the headache remedy. In action and expression she pretends to be casual and deliberately switches the line of conversation, but is seen to be still watching Judith.

ANN:
Mightn't it be more sensible to follow Michael's advice? He knows horses.

JUDITH:
>   Oh, he knows horses! So do I.

ANN:
>   Yes, but you let sentiment get in the way of common sense. Darling, the days of expensive hobbies are over. I send out the checks. I know.

Judith has finished with her teeth.

JUDITH:
>   Dad left me his colors and the horses to carry them. That's all I care about.

She starts toward the shower room.

ANN (holding out foaming salts mixture):
>   Here!

JUDITH:
>   Drink it for me, will you, dear?

She disappears into the shower room. Ann reacts, looks at the drink.

>   DISSOLVE TO:

17. EXT. LONG ISLAND COUNTRY ROAD   JUDITH'S OPEN ROADSTER
    going very fast. In the front seat are Judith and Ann. In the rumble seat is Terry.

18. FRONT SEAT   (PROCESS SHOT)   JUDITH AND ANN
    Judith, who is now wearing jodhpurs, is driving. The two are engaged in a laughing quarrel. (Jumble their speeches together.)

    ANN:
    >   You'd better let me drive.

    JUDITH:
    >   I will not.

    ANN (reaches for wheel):
    >   Here, give me—

JUDITH:
   Take your hands— (Slaps her hand.)

ANN:
   It was a gatepost you hit back there.[5]

JUDITH:
   I did not.

ANN:
   Look at your fender.

JUDITH (looks):
   Well, so I—

The car swerves.

ANN (screams):
   Hey!

JUDITH:
   Whee!

ANN:
   Well, it's a nice world—if we can just stay in it.

                                    DISSOLVE TO:

19. EXT. JUDITH'S TRAINING TRACK
     MOVING SHOT FROM JUDITH'S CAR
     with Judith and Ann in seat in foreground as car approaches the track.
        It is a half-mile training track with the infield set with hurdle jumps, not just the wooden kind, but the regular hedge jumps, a water jump—the whole works. Near the finish line there is a small uncovered bleachers. The stables immediately adjoin in back of the bleachers.
        There is the usual early morning activity, horses being run, etc. We see stable hands and, in addition, some guests who have come down to see the morning trials, including Carrie Spottswood, Colonel Mantle, and Alec Hamm.
        Near at hand is Michael. He is walking toward the track with his back to the car.

20. JUDITH AND ANN
spot Michael. Judith, with a wicked gleam in her eye, turns the car so that it is going at him. Ann realizes her intention. They smile at each other, but Ann is also a little nervous.[6]

21. SAME ANGLE AS SCENE 19
as Judith drives the car slowly up on his heels, gently bumps him with the bumper. He jumps.

MICHAEL (yells):
Hey!

Judith laughs heartily, pursues him. Michael finally manages to escape, jumps on the running board.

22. MED. CLOSE TRUCKING SHOT   THREE
as Judith drives the car alongside the track toward the people in the bleachers.

MICHAEL:
A fine way to return my call. So I managed to get you up, did I?

Angry looks between Judith and Ann.

ANN:
Michael, don't be fresh.

MICHAEL:
Now, I say if you have the finest string of horses in the country—and are proud of them—the owner—especially when she's beautiful—should come down and give the horses a look at her—if she can get up. That's one reason—[7]

Continuation of indignant looks between Ann and Judith.

JUDITH:
Well, of all the—

MICHAEL (continuing without pause):
—I called you up. Here I've got the best in the county down to see these trials—with chances for juicy sales galore— If the horses can get up early in the morning to run and jump for you, you can get up to look at them.

JUDITH (beyond endurance):
Michael!

She jams the car to a stop, throwing him off running board.

ANN:
Another word out of you—

MICHAEL:
Thanks for the lift.

He goes out.

23. ANOTHER ANGLE   JUDITH AND ANN
They are boiling over with feminine rage. They climb out of the car, walk along toward the guests during:

ANN:
I wouldn't put up with it.

JUDITH:
I won't.

ANN:
He's got to be fired.

JUDITH:
And he will be.

ANN:
Right now.

JUDITH:
Thinks he can lead us around like horses. You're right, Ann, fire him.

ANN:
> Me? Oh, no—you're the mistress—I'm only the secretary.

JUDITH:
> But, darling, you've got more character than I have—you're always telling me so yourself.[8]

Alec comes in to meet them. He is dressed in his evening clothes of the night before, including hat and topcoat.

ALEC (to Judith):
> Darling of my heart . . . Wonderful party last night.

JUDITH:
> Glad to see you're still on it, Alec.

ALEC:
> And ready for the next one . . . (Opens topcoat to show wilted flower in buttonhole.) All I've got to do is change the orchids. (To Ann.) Good morning, Ann—nice, sensible Ann.

ANN:
> Good morning, parasite. Why don't you go to bed before they put you there for good?

ALEC:
> Well, confidentially, it's a scheme. Michael said he'd give me a good fat commission if I could persuade Carrie to buy your pony, Challenger.

JUDITH:
> He didn't dare!

ALEC:
> And, frankly, I could use the cash right now.

ANN:
> This is the end!

Carrie bounces into scene.

CARRIE (to Judith):
Darling, I *will* take that colt off your hands if you'll let me have a bargain.

JUDITH:
Carrie, I won't sell you the horse—but I *will sell you his trainer!*

ALEC:
That's who she wants to buy anyway—but he won't even look at her.

CARRIE (draws herself up):
I've never heard of such a thing!

ANN (to Alec; suppressing a laugh):
Sh!

24.   ANOTHER ANGLE   JUDITH, COLONEL MANTLE, MICHAEL
as the men come up to her.

COLONEL MANTLE:
Judith, do you really want to sell that colt? Because if you do—

JUDITH:
I do not.

MICHAEL:
I think you should buy him, Colonel. He's a perfect darling. You could invite that horse to tea . . . He could play on the lawn with the dogs—or the children . . . He's a love . . . He whinnies . . . Of course, unfortunately, a steeplechaser has to have guts.

JUDITH (is burning; ignores Michael; to Colonel Mantle):
Colonel Mantle, my father held that foal up in his arms and he said, "Judy, he's a champion . . ."

Dark Victory

MICHAEL (chiming in with her):
>... "by Victory out of Field-Nurse by Man O'War. I'll call him Challenger."

JUDITH:
> Oh, I won't, I won't!

Goes out.

MICHAEL (calls after her):
> Catch him at the two-mile pole with his heart bursting and a water jump ahead and he'll fold up on you.

Ann's hand reaches into scene and whirls him around. SWING CAMERA to just Michael and Ann.

ANN:
> Michael, you might fold up and I might fold up, but that colt has the breeding.[9]

MICHAEL (smiles):
> That was for me, I take it, Miss Ann.

Judith's hand comes into scene and pulls Michael around. SWING CAMERA to just Judith and Michael.

JUDITH:
> I said I wanted to run him this morning. Where is he?

MICHAEL:
> He's in his stall having his extra forty winks before we give him his morning cup of tea.

JUDITH:
> Get him out here . . . And when I tell you to do something, you do it!

MICHAEL:
> Yes, ma'am.

He smiles and salutes her with just a shade of insolence and exits. Judith watches him and turns to rejoin Ann.

Dark Victory

A wave of dizziness hits her. She stops and puts her hand to her forehead. Ann enters scene.

ANN:
   Your head again?

JUDITH:
   It comes and goes . . . (Pause, makes up her mind to something.) I'll show him if that horse has courage. (Goes out.)

ANN (calls after her):
   Darling what are you going to do?

   DISSOLVE TO: [10]

25. EXT. INFIELD MICHAEL, JUDITH, AND CHALLENGER
   Michael is helping her up on the horse.

26. CLOSER ANGLE
   as she looks down at him. As he adjusts her foot in the stirrup he looks up at her and smiles. There is a quality in his look that strips them of their positions as a mistress and employee, reduces them to the positions of a man and a woman.

JUDITH:
   Michael, how long have I had you?

MICHAEL (promptly):
   One month— (counts) and three days.

JUDITH:
   Remind me to think about firing you.

MICHAEL (smiles significantly):
   Oh, you'll not be firing me, Miss Judith. We're going to get on together. (Back to kidding.) Now, just because I call your darling a coward—

JUDITH:
   Some day you'll learn that courage is in the blood. When any of us hits that last hurdle, it's all that counts.[11]

Dark Victory

    MICHAEL:
        Now, take your little horse and go along.

    He slaps the horse on the buttocks and it springs off at a gallop.

27.   LONG SHOT
    Judith gallops Challenger toward the first jump. Michael, watching her, walks off toward the group at the rail.

28.   PAN SHOT   JUDITH ON CHALLENGER
    approaching the first jump. They take the first jump beautifully, go on toward the second.

29.   GROUP AT RAIL   ANGLE TOWARD TRACK
    None of them are looking at Judith. Alec has their attention as he tells a story.

    ALEC:
        . . . I only arrived at four in the morning and at five the bloody butler was knocking on the door. "Are you 'unting this morning, sir?" he said . . .

    In background Judith rides in and past them.

    JUDITH (calls off):
        Hey, this is for you!

    They momentarily look at her, Colonel Mantle waves, then they turn back to Alec.

    ALEC:
        . . . "Hunting," I said. "Why, I haven't even had time to unpack my horse!"

    They all laugh.[12]

30.   LONG SHOT   JUDITH
    riding toward the second jump.

31.   MICHAEL
    watching her. There is great admiration on his face.

32. **CLOSER ANGLE   JUDITH**
   getting set for the jump. She steadies the horse.

   JUDITH:
   Easy, boy . . .

   Suddenly a great dizziness comes over her. She lowers her head and shakes it, tries to see, unconsciously pulls on the right rein.

33. **ANGLE FROM BEHIND HORSE**
   as he changes his course so that he is heading for the right wing of the jump rather than for the jump itself.

34. **MICHAEL**
   sees something is wrong.

   MICHAEL (yells):
   Look out!

35. **GROUP AT RAIL**
   turn in alarm, see Judith.

   COLONEL MANTLE:
   Great heaven, something's happened!

36. **ANN**
   looking off in fright.

   ANN:
   Hold him straight, Judy!

37. **SECOND JUMP   JUDITH ON CHALLENGER**
   drives straight for the right wing of the jump. She is still in great distress. The horse tries to jump, crashes on the wing, goes down.

38. **LONG SHOT   JUDITH AND THE COLT**
   are both on the ground. The colt is kicking wildly. Those who have been watching rush out on the infield toward her in great excitement.

   FADE OUT

FADE IN

39. INT. STALL AND STABLES MICHAEL AND A VETERINARIAN
The horse is lying in the straw on the floor as the veterinarian examines him and Michael stands by.

VET:
Except for that gash on the head, he seems to be sound.

MICHAEL:
The worse luck! (Makes a motion as if to kick the horse, stops himself.) I should have kept her off by force. I had a hunch he'd throw her.[13]

WIPE OFF TO:

40. INT. JUDITH'S BEDROOM JUDITH AND ANN
Judith is dressed to go out. She seems none the worse for the accident. She sits on the edge of her bed, drinking a cup of coffee which has been brought up on a tray.

JUDITH:
That colt didn't throw me. I threw him.

ANN:
What do you mean?

JUDITH:
Know what happened? (Grins.) I saw two jumps. I tried to put him over the wrong one.

ANN:
You saw two jumps!

JUDITH (laughs):
Yes, that was it. It was the ghastliest feeling. Everything went fuzzy.

ANN (scared):
Why didn't you tell this to Dr. Parsons?

JUDITH (chuckles):
Poor old befuddled Parsons. (Imitates him.) "My

Dark Victory

dear, you're staying up too late . . . smoking too many cigarettes . . ."

ANN:
You are, you know. These gangs of people about . . .

JUDITH (chuckles again; draws on her gloves):
If only he knew about last week at the Colony—when the old lady was coming out of the swing doors . . . I knocked the umbrella out of her hand.

ANN:
Why?

JUDITH (rattles on):
Somebody said I was drunk . . . And another time, coming out of Helene's on Park Avenue, I ran right into a woman with her dog on a leash. I ran right into the leash . . .

ANN:
Judith! You—

JUDITH:
Oh, I didn't hurt the dog—but the woman was furious. (Laughs.) Confidentially, honey, this is more than a hangover.

ANN:
If you don't tell Parsons these things, I will.

JUDITH:
No, you won't, Ann. You're my truest and best friend and you won't tell a soul. I wouldn't have told you except that I won't have a dumb animal blamed for my mistake. (Is ready; gets up.) Well, here we go. (Starts away.)

ANN:
Parsons is coming back. (Judith stops; turns in surprise.) I promised we'd go with him to a specialist—about this giddiness.

Dark Victory

JUDITH:
    I haven't time for doctors . . . (Starts again.)

ANN (follows her):
    But you may be really ill!

JUDITH:
    And I haven't time to be ill. It's just some minor nonsense.

ANN:
    If you insist on going to town you're not going without me—and have another tumble and ruin your nice clothes. You're as pigheaded as a mule! (Knock on door.) Come in!

41.   ANOTHER ANGLE   TO INCLUDE DR. PARSONS as he comes in.

PARSONS (cheerfully):
    Are we ready?

ANN:
    She says she's not going with you.

JUDITH:
    I've so much to do, darling . . . (Points to Ann.) Examine *her*. (Goes out door.)

PARSONS:
    Haven't you any influence over her?

ANN:
    None at all. (Goes to door.)

42.   STAIRWAY FROM CORRIDOR   SIDE ANGLE   JUDITH is going down out of sight.

JUDITH (gaily, as she disappears):
    Good-bye, children . . .

A second later, just as she has gone below the limit of our vision, there is a crash and the sound of her falling down the stairs.

43. IN DOORWAY   ANN
gasps in startled terror. SWING CAMERA TO ANGLE SHOOTING DOWN STAIRWAY. At the bottom of the steps Judith is lying in a heap.

FADE OUT

44. EXT. STEELE'S BROWNSTONE
A simple sign beside the door: Frederick Steele, M.D.[14]

DISSOLVE TO:

45. INT. STEELE'S WAITING ROOM   WAINWRIGHT AND STEELE
It is an old-time room which has been brightened and remodeled, yet there is a feeling of old-fashioned homeyness about it. There is considerable disorder—evidences of moving, several packing cases ready for shipping. In the foreground Wainwright is talking on the telephone. In the background Steele, his back to us, his coat off, is packing instruments in a case.

WAINWRIGHT:
I'm afraid it would be useless. Dr. Steele has closed his office . . . Permanently—yes . . . No, he's not coming back . . . You're welcome—good-bye.

STEELE (without turning):
Sounds good, eh, Wainwright?

WAINWRIGHT:
If you want to hear a fine woman break down and sob, just keep talking like that.

STEELE (laughs, comes to her):
I have to leave in forty-five minutes. Mind that, now.

WAINRIGHT:
What about this case of Dr. Parsons'? (Hands him sheaf of papers.) He's very worried—told me to keep you here, by force if necessary.

STEELE:
You tell old Parsons I've waited nine years for this

Dark Victory

train and I'm not going to miss it just because some Long Island glamour girl fell off her horse.[15] Listen to this . . . (Reads from paper.) "Miss Judith Traherne, daughter of the late sportsman and wire manufacturer . . ." Imagine putting that kind of stuff in a case history!

Taking the papers with him, he goes into

46. INT. STEELE'S CONSULTING ROOM   STEELE AND DR. CARTER

Carter has been passing the time by looking at pictures on the wall. Evidently they have been talking before. Steele tosses Judith's case history on the desk, busies himself gathering together personal belongings during:

STEELE:
Sorry, Doctor. You were saying I'm an idiot . . .

CARTER:
Exactly. Last night I was talking to the boys at the club . . . Fred, a man like you—a credit to surgery—to suddenly chuck a gold-plated practice—

STEELE:
Know much about brain surgery, Joe?

CARTER:
I know I'd be in it if I had the surgical courage. Think of it—to go inside a human being's skull and tinker with the machinery that makes the whole works go—by heaven, that's romance.

STEELE:
Romance, eh? (Hands small paper from desk to Carter.) There's your romance.

Dark Victory

CARTER (looks up in astonishment):
   This is a florist's bill.

STEELE:
   Yes. Flowers for my last patient. He was a gifted young composer. The night before the operation, he started to write a new song and— Well, maybe you read the papers . . . The operation was a brilliant success—but the patient just happened to die.[16]

CARTER:
   That's a pretty old joke.

STEELE:
   Take a look at a brain surgeon's mortality rate and find out how unfunny.

CARTER (change of tone):
   I'd never have believed it of you.

STEELE:
   Believed what?

CARTER:
   That you're quitting because you've lost your nerve. (Steele looks at him and Carter stumbles.) Well—what else is a man to think?

STEELE:
   I'm not quitting. I'm just going back into medicine.

CARTER:
   Back into medicine! Now I'm lost.

STEELE:
   I've built a small laboratory on my farm in Vermont. I'll have the backing of the Medical Research Bureau . . . Fisher in Philadelphia for the pathology—best man in the country . . . (Looks at watch.) Now, come on—

CARTER (doesn't budge):
> Don't tell me you've been bitten by the bug for scientific research?

STEELE:
> Something like that.

CARTER:
> On what?

STEELE:
> Cells. Brain cells. Why do healthy cells suddenly go berserk—grow wild? Do you know?

CARTER:
> No, I—

STEELE:
> Neither does anyone. We call them tumors—gliomas—cysts—cancers . . . We operate and try to cure with the knife when we don't even know the cause. People put their faith in us because we're doctors and— (Rings bell on desk.) Well, you can tell the boys they can split up my practice—and welcome.

On last words has pulled Carter to his feet to get him out.

CARTER:
> Well, shine my golden halo—you and Pasteur!

STEELE (taking him to door; grins):
> Probably you're right. But someday somebody's going to find a serum that will be to these growths what insulin is to diabetes—what antitoxin is to diphtheria—and really earn his title of Doctor of Medicine. (At door meets Wainwright coming in.) Wainwright, I— (Sees Parsons beyond, jumps back.) Is that Parsons?

Dark Victory

WAINWRIGHT:
    He insists.

STEELE (looks at watch):
    Well, I suppose I ought to be polite.

Wainwright goes out.

CARTER:
    So long, Fred. I'll pray for a speedy recovery. (Goes out.)

STEELE (calls after him):
    Don't hold your breath.

Parsons comes in, very agitated.

STEELE:
    I'm really sorry, Parsons, but—

PARSONS:
    Can't you put off leaving?

STEELE:
    No. I've closed my office.

PARSONS:
    Did you read the case history?

STEELE (goes to desk):
    This gossip sheet! "Daughter of the late wire manufacturer . . . !"

47.   INT. WAITING ROOM   SIDE ANGLE PAST DOOR   JUDITH AND ANN
waiting on a settee. They have overheard. Judith looks at Ann; she doesn't like Dr. Steele.

PARSONS (pokes his head out door):
    Now don't go, Judith. (Closes the door.)

JUDITH (seems impatient, but is really frightened):
    This had better be snappy. I've a date with Alec at three o'clock.

Dark Victory

ANN:
> I'm going in with you and see you don't pull the wool over his eyes.[17]

48. INT. CONSULTING ROOM STEELE AND PARSONS
Steele is looking through the case history.

PARSONS:
> I do know that girl is desperately ill. I've been watching her like a hawk—and she's been losing ground each day.

STEELE:
> If two minutes of talk will do you any good, fire ahead. What's this about headaches?

PARSONS:
> She's been having them persistently—even before the accident, I suspect.

STEELE (surprised):
> Before?

PARSONS:
> She calls them hangovers.

STEELE:
> Hm . . . (Is reading, looks up in surprise.) Three weeks! And you wait until now?

PARSONS:
> You don't know that girl . . . She's stubborn. Why, only yesterday she went to a revival of *Cyrano* in the afternoon and played bridge half the night. She won't cooperate. She won't even *tell* me anything.

STEELE (grins):
> Won't talk, eh? Well, then— (Hands Parsons case history, goes to get his coat. Parsons follows him.)

PARSONS:
> Steele, I'm an old friend of yours and I'm desperate.

Dark Victory

Why, I brought this girl into the world. I took care of her father—until he died . . .

STEELE (putting on his coat):
If she's such a crack horsewoman, why was she thrown?

PARSONS:
It was a queer sort of accident. She steered her horse into the right wing of a jump. I was there. I saw it.

STEELE (interested):
What's that? You're sure it was the right?

PARSONS:
Yes. Why?

STEELE:
Nothing . . . (Puts arm around his shoulder, takes him toward door.) Well, on the whole, I think your best bet is to get in touch with Findlay.

PARSONS:
Findlay is in Europe.

STEELE:
All right—then get Park.

PARSONS:
I don't want Park or any of the rest of them. Hang it all, they're no better than I am. I want you.

STEELE:
Can't be done.

PARSONS:
You're always talking about the obligation of doctors to humanity. Well, there's humanity waiting for you in that room.

Steele feels the reproach, then he remembers his plans and with decision opens the door.

Dark Victory

STEELE:
> Sorry, Parsons, but if I start making exceptions, I'll be stuck here another nine years. (Takes him out.)

49–53. WAITING ROOM   STEELE, PARSONS, JUDITH, ANN, WAINWRIGHT

Steele and Parsons come out of the consulting room. Judith gets up and starts out.

JUDITH:
> Come on, Ann. This is perfectly ridiculous. I'm late.

PARSONS (stops her):
> Wait, Judith. This is Dr. Steele.

JUDITH (turns, smiles):
> How do you do? My name's Traherne. (Offers hand.) Judith Traherne, or don't names matter?

STEELE (is looking at something on her hand; absently):
> Hm?

JUDITH:
> I mean, to the cold, scientific eye we're guinea pigs, aren't we? Glad to have met you, Doctor. (Turns to go.)

STEELE:
> How did you get those burns on your hand?

JUDITH (stops):
> Where?

STEELE (reaches for her hand):
> On your right hand—here—between the first two fingers.

JUDITH (looks at hand):
> I never noticed them until now.

STEELE:
> I see . . . (Draws her through doorway.) Will you just step in here, please?

Judith is surprised to find herself being led by this man. As the door closes behind them Parsons and Ann exchange a look of vast relief.

54. INT. STEELE'S CONSULTING ROOM   FULL SHOT
JUDITH AND STEELE
He is turning a chair around so that it directly faces a window through which strong sunlight streams.

STEELE:
Won't you sit here?

JUDITH (angry at being in here):
By all means, Doctor . . . I haven't much time.

STEELE:
Neither have I. (Goes to desk, rings bell.) Parsons tells me you're a great hunter.

JUDITH:
Well, you could hardly expect me to enter your office leading a pack of hounds.

This seems to stop Steele. He looks at her quickly. He just barely manages to keep from smiling. He covers up by going to Wainwright, who has come in.

55. CLOSER ANGLE   STEELE AND WAINWRIGHT

STEELE:
I'm going to have a go at this patient—but when it's time to leave, no matter what's happening, you warn me.

WAINWRIGHT:
Certainly, Doctor.

She goes out. Steele steals a look off at

56. JUDITH
watching in calm defiance.

57. WIDER ANGLE TWO
Steele gets a chair and places it so that he will face her during:

STEELE:
I understand you don't like to talk about your health?

JUDITH:
I don't.

STEELE:
Any reason why?

JUDITH:
It's a boring topic, that's all.

STEELE:
Most people love it. I make my living by listening to them.

JUDITH:
Then I'm afraid you're wasting your time.

STEELE (sits):
Oh, I'll send you a bill.

JUDITH (rapidly and flatly, as if she's reciting a lesson):
I'm twenty-three years old. An only child. I weigh one hundred and fifteen pounds—stripped. I've had mumps, measles, and whooping cough, all at the proper ages. I believe I have no congenital weaknesses. Shall I go on?

STEELE:
Yes, please.

JUDITH (as before):
My father drank himself to death; my mother lives in Paris. I take a great deal of exercise. I'm accustomed to a reasonable quantity of tobacco and alcohol. I'm said to have a sense of humor. Is that all?

Dark Victory

STEELE:
　All the inconsequential facts.

She tries to light a cigarette but misses the end of it with the match. He guides her hand.

JUDITH:
　What are the consequential ones?

STEELE (as if changing the subject; indicates window):
　Does that light bother you? (Makes move to rise.)

JUDITH:
　No. (Steele settles back.)

STEELE:
　Do you use your eyes a great deal?

JUDITH:
　I generally keep them open, Doctor.

That seems to stop Steele again. He gets up.

58.　WIDER ANGLE　TWO
as Steele goes to his desk and gets a cigarette. He walks around, pretending not to pay much attention to her, but in reality studying her intently during:

STEELE (chattily):
　What on earth do you do with yourself down there on Long Island?

JUDITH:
　Oh, horses, dogs—shooting—yachting—parties—travel—gossip—all the pleasures of the station wagon crowd— You don't think much of that, do you?

STEELE:
　No. Not much.

JUDITH:
　Why not?

STEELE:
> It just doesn't appeal to me.

JUDITH:
> Do you condemn everything that doesn't appeal to you, Dr. Steele?

STEELE:
> By no means . . . you asked for my opinion—and I gave it.

JUDITH:
> Well, anyway, that's my racket. What's yours?

STEELE:
> High pressure surgery—Park Avenue clientele—about ten days off each summer.

JUDITH:
> Sounds perfectly awful.

STEELE:
> It is.

JUDITH:
> Then why do you do it?

STEELE:
> Because, like you, I've been caught in a racket.

JUDITH:
> Oh, Doctor, what a relief to know you're no better than I am.

STEELE:
> Ah! But I'm leaving my racket. I'm clearing out for northern Vermont in— (looks at watch) fifteen minutes.

JUDITH:
> Vermont? You don't mean that narrow little pinched-up state on the wrong side of Boston?

STEELE:
: That's the one!

JUDITH:
: No kidding?

STEELE:
: No kidding.

JUDITH:
: What are you going to do there—between yawns?

STEELE:
: You wouldn't be interested.

JUDITH:
: Come now. After leading me on like this . . .

STEELE:
: I'm going to do scientific research on the growth of cells.

JUDITH (wickedly):
: In guinea pigs?

STEELE:
: No, just cells.

JUDITH:
: Sounds silly.

STEELE:
: So I'm told.

JUDITH (repentant):
: Still—I almost envy you—it must be nice to believe in what you're doing.

STEELE:
: Don't you?

JUDITH:
: Not in the way you do. Oh, I'm not complaining . . . take it all in all, they dealt me a very good

hand. I'm young—I have no particular responsibilities—I shan't cultivate them, either—one is freer without. I shall probably marry someday—no hurry about that. When I do, I shall build a house on a ridge I know—with a glorious view. I'll have my horses—with luck I'll have about forty years of it. I think that's a pretty good setup.

STEELE:
That light *is* in your eyes.

He goes to the window and lowers the shade.

JUDITH:
I wish you wouldn't keep harping on that. There's nothing the matter with my eyes.

STEELE:
You're squinting.

JUDITH:
I'm not squinting!

STEELE:
There. That's better.

59.   MED. SHOT   JUDITH
stamps out her cigarette.

JUDITH:
Suit yourself. It's your office.

Steele enters scene.

STEELE:
What did you do yesterday?

JUDITH:
I played bridge in the afternoon. I went to the theater in the evening.

STEELE:
Other way around, wasn't it?

JUDITH:
> Why . . . yes. I guess it was.

STEELE:
> What was the play?

JUDITH:
> Er . . .

STEELE:
> *Cyrano,* wasn't it?

JUDITH:
> Yes, why?

STEELE:
> Did you like it?

JUDITH:
> My head was aching so—

STEELE:
> How long have you had these headaches?

JUDITH:
> Oh, I . . . I don't have them.

STEELE:
> You have one now.

JUDITH:
> No! I have not!

STEELE:
> How did you come out at bridge yesterday?

JUDITH:
> Let me think . . .

STEELE:
> Quickly!

JUDITH:
> I don't remember.

Dark Victory

STEELE:
> I know, you lost.

JUDITH:
> Yes, I lost.

STEELE:
> How much?

JUDITH:
> How can I remember? I play bridge every day . . .

STEELE:
> You've been losing a lot lately, haven't you?

JUDITH:
> Yes . . .

STEELE:
> Playing badly?

JUDITH:
> I—

STEELE:
> Forgetting what cards are out and what's the bid?

JUDITH (angrily):
> Why do you ask me those stupid questions? (Starts to get up.)

STEELE (holds her down):
> Wait! Did Parsons say you could go out yesterday?

JUDITH:
> I'm accustomed to looking after myself.

STEELE:
> But you did disobey his orders, didn't you?

JUDITH:
> What if I did?

STEELE:
> Why pay a doctor to advise you and then disregard his advice?

Dark Victory

JUDITH:
I didn't call him! Someone else called him.

STEELE:
So you're taking orders from someone else, aren't you?

JUDITH (throws his hand off her shoulder):
Listen, Doctor. I've never taken orders from anyone and as long as I live I shall never take orders—from anyone. And here's something else. I'm well, absolutely well! I'm young and strong and nothing can touch me—neither you nor Dr. Parsons can make an invalid out of me. And now I'm going. (Rises.)

60. WIDER ANGLE   TWO
as Judith goes toward door.

JUDITH:
I'm sorry to have wasted so much of your time, but this is my last interview with doctors!

STEELE:
That's right! Run away because you're frightened!

JUDITH (whirls):
That isn't true!

STEELE:
Oh, yes it is.

He goes to her.

61. CLOSE SHOT   TWO
as he enters to her. She listens to him defiantly as he hands her the truth.

STEELE (with calm, methodical brutality):
That's why you held certain things back from Dr. Parsons. You were afraid to admit them. You didn't tell him that you've been having those headaches for months—but you have and they've been getting

worse lately until now you're never free of them. And your eyes have been cutting up, too—just as though someone were shutting a pair of folding doors—until your vision is almost cut in half. You pretended it was imagination, but it isn't. Then that queer dull feeling in your right arm. You couldn't laugh that off. I'll tell you how you got those burns—a cigarette! It burned your fingers and you never felt it because your tactile nerves are paralyzed.[18] Your memory is all shot to pieces. You can't concentrate. Look at your bridge scores! You're irritable because your nerves are all on edge. You're afraid to admit it, but you can't deny it!

JUDITH:
It's a lie! I'm well! Why do you bully me like this?[19]

STEELE (quietly):
Because I want to help you.

Judith looks away from him, down at the floor. She is terribly shaken. There is quite a long pause, then slowly she walks out of scene, away from the door. He watches her and we know that he is feeling sorry that he has had to use brutality.

62. WIDER ANGLE TWO
Judith slowly goes to another chair or a couch in the room and sits down.

STEELE:
Thank you. (He goes to his desk.) Now we can get somewhere.

He rings the bell on the desk, then picks up a chair, and goes to Judith. He sits down facing her, quite close to her.

63. MED. CLOSE ANGLE TWO
Judith is fighting gamely for her control against the fear

Dark Victory

that, once admitted, threatens to overwhelm her. Steele's manner is very gentle.

STEELE:
> Just give me your right hand, please . . . Now the left . . . Now squeeze—tight—good and tight . . . Thank you.

Wainwright enters with a table on which there is a tray of instruments and places it by his elbow.

STEELE (to Judith):
> Would you mind removing your coat, please?

As he helps her off with it . . .

WAINWRIGHT:
> It's nearly time, Doctor.

STEELE (to Wainwright; abstractedly):
> Yes, yes—thanks. (To Judith.) Just give me your right elbow, please, in my hand.

He sits down and takes her elbow in his hand. Wainwright goes out.

STEELE:
> Just relax—Good. (Tests with reflex hammer.) Now the other one. Good. (Repeats test.) Cross your knees, please. (Tests with hammer.)

JUDITH (a small laugh):
> That always makes me laugh.

STEELE:
> Silly, isn't it? Now the other one. (Repeats knee test.) Good. Good. (Takes ophthalmoscope from tray.) Now don't be frightened at this. It's just an electric torch.

JUDITH (quietly):
> You're very kind to your guinea pigs, aren't you?

STEELE (smiles):
> Would you mind just looking straight ahead, please?

64. CLOSER ANGLE   JUDITH   OVER HIS SHOULDER
as he examines her right eye with the ophthalmoscope. He examines her pupil, sees defect, becomes thoughtful.

STEELE:
> Hm . . .

JUDITH:
> I've been told they're a nice color.

(NOTE: In this scene her kidding is no longer defiance—rather, whistling in the dark.)

STEELE (smiles):
> Just once again. (Examines pupil again, then shifts over and examines other eye.) Steady. (Puts ophthalmoscope on tray, takes up a small cube.)

JUDITH:
> Do you agree?

STEELE (preoccupied):
> Hm?

JUDITH:
> About the color of my eyes . . .

STEELE:
> Oh, yes—fine. Would you mind closing them for a minute. Hold out both hands with the palms upward. (Puts cube in her left hand.) Can you tell me what that is?

JUDITH:
> It's a cube.

STEELE:
> Is it hard or soft?

Dark Victory

JUDITH:
   Hard.

STEELE (transfers cube to her right hand):
   Now what's this?

JUDITH:
   I'm not quite sure.

STEELE (substitutes pencil for cube):
   What's this? Turn it over in your fingers . . . What shape is it?

JUDITH:
   I can't quite make out.

STEELE (places pencil in her left hand):
   Now. Can you tell me what this is?

JUDITH:
   A pencil, silly.

STEELE:
   Right.

JUDITH:
   Can I open my eyes now?

STEELE:
   No. Just a minute. (Puts a piece of silk in her left hand.) Is that cloth rough or smooth?

JUDITH:
   It's a piece of silk.

STEELE:
   I'm going to fool you this time. Now what's this? (Substitutes a piece of burlap in her right hand.)

JUDITH:
   You can't fool me—still silk.

STEELE (puts burlap back on tray):
   You can open your eyes now.

JUDITH:
> Do I get promoted, teacher?

STEELE:
> Now, just uncross your knees, please. Sit up straight, please. I'm going to hold out my hands like this . . . (stretches out both his arms) and ask you to close one eye. Then I will move my hands in and I want you to stop me quickly when they come within your line of vision. Will you mind closing your left eye—that's it, just cup it—don't press— and stop me very quickly with this hand— (indicates her right hand) when you see my hands moving in. Ready?

Again he stretches out his arms and slowly moves his hands in until they come within her range of vision. She can't see to the right and therefore fails to see the approach of his left hand.

STEELE:
> Now again—the same with the other eye. Ready. (Repeats the same business.) Good. That's all.[20]

He rises.

65. WIDER ANGLE TWO

STEELE:
> Just two more question. How long ago did you first notice these headaches?

JUDITH:
> Horrible months ago. Five or six.

STEELE:
> Have your eyes bothered you as long as that?

JUDITH:
> No. That's only lately. The last few weeks.

Dark Victory

STEELE:
> That's a great help. (Tap on door.) Now I'm going to ask you—

He stops as Wainwright comes in.

WAINWRIGHT:
> Dr. Steele, you'll have to leave this minute if you're going to catch your train.

STEELE:
> Train! (Looks at watch. Long pause.) Yes, I suppose I will.[21]

He looks at Judith.

66. CLOSE-UP JUDITH
is looking at him as if her last prop has gone out from under her. There is frightened appeal in her eyes.

67. GROUP
Judith and Steele continue to look at each other, then she looks away.

JUDITH:
> It's my own fault I didn't come to you sooner.

STEELE (makes her decision; to Wainwright):
> Miss Wainwright—there are other trains on other days.

WAINWRIGHT:
> Doctor!

Judith looks up at him with vast relief.

STEELE (sternly):
> Cancel the tickets.

WAINWRIGHT:
> Yes, Doctor.

She hurries out. Judith gets up and comes to him.

JUDITH:
>Thank you.

STEELE:
>Not at all. A few days one way or the other won't matter.

JUDITH:
>I'm sorry I was so difficult.

STEELE:
>I like the way you fought back at me. You've been a good sport.

JUDITH:
>If I weren't that, Doctor, I'm afraid I wouldn't be much of anything. What's wrong with me? Is it my eyes?

STEELE:
>I'd be a poor excuse for a doctor if I told you before I'm positive myself. For the next few days I'm going to ask you to have some X rays taken—lots of them. Otherwise you're to live your normal life—do everything you've been doing—see your friends—have parties—everything the same—with one exception . . .

JUDITH:
>What's that?

STEELE:
>You'll have to see a good deal of me.

JUDITH (smiles):
>I'll bet you'll be a frost at a party.

>>FADE OUT

FADE IN

68. INT. JUDITH'S LOWER HALLWAY   CLOSE SHOT   TABLE
on which three men's hats are lying side by side. From the playroom, off-scene, we hear the sound of music

Dark Victory

from a phonograph, laughter and chatter from a crowd of people.

DISSOLVE TO:

69. INT. JUDITH'S BEDROOM   JUDITH, STEELE, AND TWO SPECIALISTS

Steele and the two other doctors—three tall figures—are grouped around a large wing chair in which Judith is sitting. She is a small, pathetic figure. She is very quiet and not as cheeky as she has been. She wears a dressing gown, and her feet are bare. One of the doctors is repeating the sight test which Steele used in his office. He looks at Steele and nods.

JUDITH:
   So what, gentlemen?

FIRST SPECIALIST:
   If you'll put your clothes on we'll go in here.[22] (Indicates sitting room.)

As the three doctors file toward the sitting room

JUDITH:
   If you care to smoke, you'll find cigarettes on the table.

She hears a burst of laughter from downstairs and runs out the door to the corridor.

70. STAIRWAY   JUDITH

runs partway down, bare feet and all, stops, and calls into playroom.

JUDITH (gaily):
   Be quiet, you guys—we've got doctors in the house.

71. PLAYROOM DOOR   FROM HER PERSPECTIVE

Alec appears in doorway. Behind him we see the gang in for cocktails—Alec, Carrie, Colonel Mantle. Ann is there.

97

Dark Victory

ALEC:
What have you got?

72. FULL SHOT   HALL

JUDITH:
I don't know yet. Maybe it's kittens.

She turns and sees the two specialists coming downstairs.

JUDITH:
Well—what's the verdict?

FIRST SPECIALIST:
Dr. Steele will talk to you.

ANN:
I'll show the doctors out.

JUDITH:
Right. Then come up. Thanks, gentlemen.

She runs upstairs two steps at a time.

73. ANN
watching her, troubled and worried.

74. INT. JUDITH'S SITTING ROOM   STEELE AND JUDITH
Steele is sitting in a chair, smoking and thinking, not relishing the job ahead of him. He doesn't hear Judith as she comes in from behind him. Because she is frightened, she kids as she stands before him.

JUDITH:
The prisoner will rise. The sentence.

Steele has risen during her speech.

STEELE:
We will have to operate.

JUDITH:
> What do you mean—operate? On me? Where? (He touches her head.) No!

STEELE:
> After all, the brain is like any other part of the body. Things get out of kilter—have to be adjusted.

JUDITH:
> I won't . . . Ann! (Runs to door, opens it, calls.) Ann!

75. CLOSER ANGLE   JUDITH
looks off in fright at Steele.

ANN'S VOICE (alarmed):
> What's the matter?

JUDITH (motioning frantically):
> Come here!

Ann runs in. Judith takes her hand, pulls her out toward Steele.

76. WIDER ANGLE   THREE

JUDITH:
> Tell her! He wants to operate!

ANN:
> Operate?

JUDITH:
> On my head!

ANN (to Steele):
> Oh, you've made a mistake!

STEELE:
> I knew almost at once . . . but I wanted confirmation . . .

The two girls are clinging to each other for support. They are panic-stricken—two frightened children.

Dark Victory

ANN:
> What's she got?

JUDITH:
> What *have* I got?

STEELE:
> The technical name is glioma.[23]

JUDITH:
> Glioma?

ANN:
> Don't listen to him!

JUDITH:
> It sounds like a kind of plant.

STEELE:
> Yes—it is rather like a plant—a parasitic one. If it's removed . . .

ANN:
> All surgeons are alike. Don't get upset, Judith. You wait—call in other doctors . . .

JUDITH:
> Yes, yes, of course.

STEELE:
> You've got to face it sooner or later.

JUDITH:
> Suppose we don't talk about it anymore.[24] (Goes toward dressing room.)

STEELE:
> Just as you like. Good-bye. (Starts away.)

ANN:
> Glioma?

STEELE:
> It's not as serious as it sounds—it's just the idea that's hard to get used to.

Dark Victory

77. INT. JUDITH'S DRESSING ROOM   JUDITH AND MARTHA
    The maid is placing freshly ironed clothes in the wardrobe as Judith comes in. Judith closes the door, leans back against it, a terrible fear gripping her. Martha watches her and says nothing.

    JUDITH (calls):
       Ann, ask the doctor to wait. Get him some champagne.

    She goes to a chair before a mirror and sits down.

78. CLOSER ANGLE   JUDITH IN MIRROR
    She places both hands to her forehead, pulls back her hair. We see the reflection of Martha as she comes to her.

    MARTHA:
       Another headache, Miss Judith?

    JUDITH:
       No, not another headache . . . Yes, a big headache! And I'm going to have a nice big bottle of champagne for it . . .

                                              FADE OUT [25]

79–82. OMITTED

83. HOSPITAL CORRIDOR   TRUCKING SHOT   ANN, JUDITH, AND ALEC WITH MARTHA
    following are walking toward Judith's room, looking at the numbers on the doors.

    ALEC (chattering):
       This seems insane! I mean to walk into this joint on your feet. I knew a man once—a nice guy—walked in like this and went out feet first.

    ANN (kicks him):
       Will you be quiet!

JUDITH:
> Here we are—four twenty-six. (Taps on door.)

ALEC:
> I tell you—I'll get you off to a good start—I'll flirt with your nurse.

The door is opened by Miss Dodd.

MISS DODD:
> I am Miss Dodd.

ALEC (gets one look at her):
> Oh!

84. INT. HOSPITAL ROOM   FULL SHOT
as they all come in. We keep Alec and Miss Dodd in foreground chattering. Martha methodically goes about the business of unpacking. In the background Judith and Ann walk through room, looking around at the strange surroundings—already beginning to be frightened—go to a window, and look out and down

ALEC:
> How do you do, Miss Dodd—of the Virginia Dodds? My name's Hamm—of the Westphalian Hamms. We're terribly sorry to be late . . . some people dropped in . . .

85. AT WINDOW   JUDITH AND ANN
They are both contemplating the fact that Judith is definitely in the hospital, and they feel danger closing in on them. OVER THE SCENE comes Alec's chatter.

ALEC'S VOICE:
> Then of course I managed to get a little tight—so I had to be revived—to be brought along for moral support.

JUDITH (uncertainly):
> Well . . . I've got a nice view.

Dark Victory

ANN:
>Darling, it's not too—

She checks herself from adding "late" when she sees that Judith is suffering an attack of dizziness and realizes the serious thing that has brought them here.

86. WIDER ANGLE   WHOLE GROUP

MISS DODD (to Alec):
>I must ask you to step outside now because I must get the patient to bed. She was due at two o'clock—and the doctor has left quite a few orders.

ALEC:
>Sorry . . . I'll blow. Good-bye, kids.

Judith crosses the room, takes his hand.

JUDITH (with front of bravery):
>Good-bye, Alec. Tell everybody I'm going to be fine— Call me tomorrow . . .

87. CLOSE-UP   ANN
for her reaction.

ALEC'S VOICE:
>Chin up. They won't hurt my Judith.

88. FULL SHOT   WHOLE GROUP
Alec goes out. Now the machinery of the hospital starts. Miss Dodd comes forward to Judith.

MISS DODD:
>We're late . . . we've lots to do . . . Doctor's orders must be followed. (Looks at her watch.)

JUDITH (almost irritably):
>Well . . . what first?

MISS DODD:
>We'll just get your things off and pop you into bed.

Dark Victory

JUDITH (looks at hospital bed):
> Into that?

MISS DODD:
> Yes.

JUDITH:
> Right now?

MISS DODD:
> If you don't mind.

JUDITH:
> Well— (To Martha.) Give me my nightdress and things—quickly.

Miss Dodd brings a regulation hospital garb that has been lying on the bed, takes the nightie from Judith's hand, and hands her the hospital garb.

MISS DODD:
> No, we won't have those . . . we're going to wear these.

JUDITH:
> What are they? Can't I wear my own nightie? (Takes pants part of outfit, holds them up against herself, looks up in horror.) Am I operated on in these?

MISS DODD (patiently):
> Just slip them on, please.

JUDITH (holds coat of outfit to shoulders, looks at it, looks at Ann):
> Ann! Look! (Tries to make joke of it.) The latest from Paris—strictly clinical.

ANN:
> If you have to get them on—get them on.

Judith clonks down on the side of the bed and looks around the room. She is bewildered. The panicky desire to escape is overwhelming her.

Dark Victory

JUDITH:
: Where's Dr. Steele?

MISS DODD:
: In the building . . .

JUDITH:
: Do you think you could find him for me?

MISS DODD:
: I'll try. (Goes to telephone.)

JUDITH:
: Ann . . .

Ann comes to her.

MISS DODD (on phone):
: Flash Dr. Steele for room four twenty-six, please.

89. CLOSER ANGLE   JUDITH AND ANN
They are both in a panic.

JUDITH:
: I want to go home!

ANN:
: Well, if I'd had my way—

                          WIPE OFF TO:

90–91. HOSPITAL CORRIDOR   INSERT   FLASHER
flashing Steele's number: 111—111.[26]

92–94. INT. HOSPITAL ROOM   FULL SHOT   JUDITH, MISS DODD, AND STEELE
The latter comes in and goes directly to the bed where Judith is sitting up stiffly and uncomfortably as if she didn't belong there. From the moment of his entrance we notice that Ann watches him steadily. It is clear that she resents him because he represents the things that are threatening Judith.

Dark Victory

STEELE:
> How is everything?

JUDITH:
> Everything's awful. Look what you make me wear— (Indicating hospital garment.)

STEELE (grins):
> Pretty dowdy, aren't they? I suppose you brought a lot of nice things of your own?

JUDITH:
> Of course I did. I have lovely nighties. I bought two new ones especially for—this.

Steele looks at Ann, who looks back at him without a sign of friendliness. He looks back at Judith, then at the nurse.

STEELE:
> Miss Dodd, I see no reason why Miss Traherne shouldn't wear something of her own.

JUDITH:
> They're in the drawer.

Steele goes to the dresser. Ann watches him as he picks up something from the drawer—possibly a very nice negligee—brings it to the bed.

JUDITH:
> Well—turn your head.

STEELE (with a look at the nurse):
> Suppose we don't put it on . . . suppose we just tuck it around you—for the effect. (He drapes it around her.) Better?

JUDITH:
> Much.

Miss Dodd, who has been waiting with the pill and glass of water, now brings it forward. Steele takes it.

Dark Victory

JUDITH (suspicously):
: What's that?

STEELE:
: Something to make you sleep.

He offers it to her. She hesitates, takes it, pops it into her mouth, takes a sip of water.

JUDITH:
: I don't want to go to sleep. How could anyone sleep in a two-by-four thing like this? At home I have a bed big enough for six—and here I can't move.

STEELE:
: Now wait a minute . . . (Ann is still watching.) I'll show you something about this bed . . . (Goes to foot of bed; Ann is in his way.) Pardon me . . . (She moves aside; he turns foot crank.) It goes up to rest your legs . . . (Turns head crank.) And up and down to make your back feel better. Before you're through, you'll want to take it home with you.

95. CLOSER ANGLE TWO

as Judith settles down in bed. She sighs sleepily. The drug is beginning to take effect.

JUDITH (looks up at him):
: You do make it feel better. (Pause.) You know, I can't understand me— I've never given in a fraction to anyone else, and here I am letting you bounce me up and bounce me down . . . In fact, I'm letting you—(A little return of panic.) Exactly where— where does it happen— (Feels her head.) Here— here . . . ?

STEELE:
: That's my worry.

JUDITH:
: How do you do it? Just what do you do?

STEELE:
> Chatterbox, aren't you?

JUDITH:
> Ugh. It's very distasteful, isn't it? Oh, well, I don't care. (Sighs sleepily.) I don't care about anything. This is such a nice bed . . . and it's a nice room, too. Thank you, Ann. Ann, you're standing over there miles away—come over here . . .

96.   THE THREE
as Ann goes to her. Judith takes her hand.

JUDITH (to Ann):
> I love you. I don't know what I'd do without you.

ANN (under her breath; very quietly):
> I love you.

JUDITH (to both):
> Do you like each other?

STEELE:
> Of course.

ANN (noncommittally):
> Sure.

JUDITH (very drowsily):
> I want you to like each other. I love everybody . . . (Suddenly sits up straight with a terrifying thought.) Will they cut off my hair?

STEELE:
> Just a little of it—

Ann turns and walks hastily out of scene.

JUDITH:
> I don't want my hair cut off!

STEELE:
> It will grow back.

Dark Victory

JUDITH (sinks back on pillow feeling appeased):
    Yes, of course it will . . . Silly of me. (Sighs.) I feel so good. Nothing to think about . . .

STEELE:
    You're going to sleep now.

CAMERA STARTS MOVING UP SLOWLY TOWARD HER.

JUDITH (very drowsily):
    That's right . . . I must do everything you say . . . (Reaches out and takes his hands.) I'm in your hands . . . They're nice hands . . . They're good strong hands . . . Doctor?

STEELE'S VOICE:
    Yes?

JUDITH:
    When you get inside my head—see if you can find any sense in it.

CAMERA CONTINUES TO MOVE UP and the scene goes fuzzy.[27]

                                              FADE OUT

FADE IN

97.   CORRIDOR   OUTSIDE SURGERY
In the background we see enough set to indicate busy operating rooms. To one side of these there is a door which leads into the doctors' dressing room. Near at hand against the wall there is a tiny switchboard—a little call telephone with about six or eight plugs—with phones on top. A nice little secretary is working at it.

SECRETARY:
    St. Mary's Hospital—Doctors' Room—Surgery—Yes, I'll tell him.

Dr. Driscoll enters scene and goes toward doctors' dressing room. CAMERA FOLLOWS HIM.

Dark Victory

SECRETARY:
> Dr. Steele—Yes, Dr. Steele is all through in Surgery Seven—it's all clear . . .

By now we are going through the door into the doctors' dressing room. There is the activity of many doctors, as before. In the background, not obvious to us at first, is Steele, at a wash basin, washing his hands and staring straight ahead, oblivious to everything around him. Nearby, watching him, is Dr. Parsons.

As the CAMERA FOLLOWS Dr. Driscoll, we PICK UP snatches of ad libs from the other doctors on the fly.

AD LIBS:
> What did you shoot? Ninety-two. My putting was way off. I saw you with that girl. It wasn't bad—a simple carcinoma. It was a good game until the ninth inning. Etc., etc.[28]

Parsons sees Driscoll, comes a few steps to meet him. His expression is one of a man who has been shaken by a bad blow. CAMERA REMAINS ON THEM, but in the background we clearly see Steele deep in his troubled thoughts.

PARSONS:
> Dr. Driscoll, was that the laboratory's last word? Is there no hope at all in the pathological findings?

DRISCOLL:
> I'm afraid not, Parsons. She's bound to get a recurrence.

PARSONS:
> And that means . . . ?

DRISCOLL:
> About ten months, I'd guess.

PARSONS:
> Invalidism, I suppose?

Dark Victory

DRISCOLL:
> No. I'd say it's a rare case. She'll apparently be as well as any of us—that is until—well, her sight may fail near the end.

PARSONS:
> Amblyopia?

DRISCOLL:
> Yes. There'll be only a few hours after that.

PARSONS:
> Hang it, Steele—don't stand there saying nothing!

STEELE:
> Rotten business, doctoring.

A DOCTOR (from basin next to Steele):
> What's the matter, Steele?

STEELE (hating the word):
> A glioma! (Turns to Parsons.) A girl like that—who is so alive—and so entitled to live . . . to have this contemptible, meaningless growth come along and put a period to it! You could almost wish—it had happened on the table . . .

PARSONS:
> Are you going to tell her?

STEELE:
> Would you want her to know?

PARSONS:
> . . . No.

STEELE:
> Then that's the answer. Come on.

98. TRUCKING SHOT
The CAMERA FOLLOWING them back through room of doctors. More ad libs and laughter.

Dark Victory

AD LIBS:
> The food's all right, if you like Italian cooking. Just wait until state medicine comes in . . . then we can quit when the whistle blows. Boy, I feel good!

DISSOLVE TO:

99. CORRIDOR OUTSIDE JUDITH'S ROOM   ALEC AND STEELE
Steele comes toward Judith's room. He is preoccupied and stern. Alec gets up from the chair beside Judith's door, motions as if to speak to him—a pathetic gesture. Steele goes by without seeing him into Judith's room.[29]

100. INT. HOSPITAL ROOM
The shades are drawn. The room is in shadows. Judith is breathing evenly—still unconscious. Miss Dodd is watching her. Ann is seated in a chair in a corner. As Steele comes in she watches him anxiously but doesn't move.[30] Steele seems not to see her. He goes to the bed and looks down at Judith, then goes to the chart and examines it.

STEELE:
> Watch her temperature. I'll be back later.

101. ANN
watching anxiously. She gets up. CAMERA PANS her to him. She looks up at him, not daring to ask. After a moment:

STEELE (without looking at her):
> She'll be all right.

ANN:
> How long . . .

STEELE:
> A few weeks' convalescence.

ANN:
> Will she really be all right—as she was before?

STEELE:
I think so, yes.

He turns and CAMERA PANS HIM OUT of the room.

102. ANN
There has been something about his manner—the way he has spoken—which makes her suspect that something is more wrong than he admits. She follows him out.

103. CORRIDOR   OUTSIDE JUDITH'S ROOM   STEELE, ANN, AND ALEC
From the chair, Alec watches Ann come out of the room, run down the corridor after Steele, and catch him by the arm.

ANN:
You *think* so!

STEELE (strongly):
I can promise a complete surgical recovery.

ANN:
What does that mean? *Will she be well?*

STEELE:
. . . Yes.

Steele turns on his heel and walks away. As she watches him go her face says, "I think you're lying."[31]

FADE OUT

104–113. OMITTED

FADE IN

114. INT. JUDITH'S BEDROOM   JUDITH, ANN, ALEC, AND MARTHA
Judith is at a mirror with her back to us. Assisted by Martha, she is putting on a hat. Ann and Alec are watching, the latter sprawled in a chair with a drink in his

Dark Victory

hand. Off-scene from the grounds outside the windows, we hear someone signaling to attract attention. This is repeated periodically throughout the scene, but no one seems to notice it much except Ann.

JUDITH (without turning around):
Look—it fits beautifully—doesn't it, Ann?

ANN:
It's lovely.

JUDITH:
You couldn't tell a thing, could you? Aren't they marvelous these days?

ALEC:
Do you mind turning around? I'm tired of this vista.

Ann goes to the door which leads out to balcony to investigate the whistle.

JUDITH (dismissing Martha):
Thank you, Martha. That's very good. (Turns around.) Behold—a new woman—from top to bottom. (Showing off.) New shoes—new stockings—new dress—new head . . .

ALEC:
And certainly a new disposition.

JUDITH:
What was wrong with my old one?

ALEC:
Never mind, pet. I always loved you despite your faults.

ANN (comes back from window):
Judith, if you don't do something, I will. It's that Michael.

JUDITH:
What does he think he's doing? Whistling at us!

Dark Victory

They both go to the balcony door.

ALEC (gets up and goes out):
　I'm going down and herald your coming.

JUDITH (as she opens door):
　Now, Ann, you fire him . . .

She pushes her out the door. Follows.

115.　BALCONY OUTSIDE JUDITH'S ROOM
　　　Judith and Ann come out.

ANN:
　Michael, what sort of manners—

JUDITH:
　Look, Ann. It's Challenger!

116.　FROM THEIR PERSPECTIVE   MICHAEL AND CHALLENGER
　　　Michael has ridden the horse to the house but has now dismounted and is looking up and grinning.

MICHAEL:
　And it's Michael, too.

117.　MASTER SHOT   WHOLE GROUP

JUDITH:
　How nice to bring him, Michael.

MICHAEL:
　Well, your little horse was exercising me, so I thought you might like to have a look at us.

ANN:
　Run along. You whistle like a peanut wagon.

JUDITH:
　Well, he's looking *fine*. Look at that coat, Ann. How's he going, Michael?

Dark Victory

MICHAEL:
> Oh, beautifully! I'm teaching him to crochet. He's working on a set of doilies.

JUDITH:
> Of all the cheek! You'll eat those words when he wins the Grand National next spring.

MICHAEL:
> Women are stubborn. I hoped what the doctor did to your head would make you more sensible.[32]

JUDITH:
> Now don't get fresh with me, Michael. I'm back, and I'm full of vim and vigor, and I'll cut you down!

MICHAEL (more serious):
> How do you feel—really?

JUDITH:
> Well, how do I look?

MICHAEL:
> Fine from here. I'd like to see you a little closer . . .

ANN:
> That barnyard Romeo! (To Michael.) Go back to the stables and get a broom!

118.   MICHAEL

His true feelings come rather awkwardly through his customary air of kidding.

MICHAEL:
> Well, kidding on the level—I want to tell you that everything around here—the boys at the stable—Well, there was a general sigh of relief. (He raises his cap, and he does it beautifully.) I'm very glad . . . !

He turns back to the horse, a little flustered, and quickly prepares to be off.

119. JUDITH AND ANN

    JUDITH:
        Thanks for bringing him, Michael.

They watch him ride away—SOUND EFFECT of horse galloping.

    ANN (calls after him):
        Next time let the horse ride you—you donkey!

Judith is looking about over her grounds as if seeing the world anew and relishing it. She draws in a deep breath of fresh air.

    JUDITH:
        Doesn't the world *smell* nice, Ann?

    ANN:
        What Michael said was right—all the servants—everybody for miles around—are thrilled that you're back with us.

She puts her arm around Judith's waist and hugs her. There is a moment of perfect and loving understanding between the two.

    JUDITH:
        It's nice to be loved. (Pause; change to lighter tone.) Where *is* that New England quack?

    ANN (gives her quick look):
        I told him five o'clock. (Looks down drive.) Is that his car turning in now?

    JUDITH (quickly):
        Come on!

She drags Ann inside.

120. INT. JUDITH'S BEDROOM PAN SHOT JUDITH AND ANN come from the balcony, start through the room running. Judith stops and runs back to the mirror.

JUDITH:
>Do I look all right . . . ? Or shall I change my hat again?

ANN (takes her hand, pulls her toward corridor door):
>It used to be six hats on the floor—now it's twelve . . . You used to be mad but—I don't know what that doctor's done to you—you're madder still now . . .

By which time they are well out of the room.

121. STAIRWAY PAN SHOT JUDITH AND ANN
coming down rapidly, arm in arm.

JUDITH:
>Now, let's not make a fuss over him—and spoil him . . . I'm going to be very busy with my friends . . . I'm not going to seem anxious . . . Now, don't you be too anxious, Ann . . .

By which time they have reached the foot of the stairs and have gone into:

122. INT. PLAYROOM PAN SHOT JUDITH AND ANN
FOLLOW THEM as Judith greets various friends. In the shifting background we see that the gang is here—having cocktails, chatter and laughter, music, backgammon.

JUDITH:
>Hi!

CARRIE:
>Judith, darling! You've never looked better.

JUDITH:
>Thanks, Carrie.

CARRIE:
>How did you manage about the hair?

JUDITH:
> I'm not telling.

Colonel Mantle picks her up for a few steps, takes her arm.

COLONEL MANTLE:
> It's good, honey—really good . . . This blasted house has been a morgue.

Judith pats his hand.

JUDITH (to Ann):
> Has he come in?

ANN (looks back):
> No.

JUDITH:
> Let's have some champagne. He said I could. Let's not wait. (Gets champagne at bar.) Have one, Ann. (Toasts.) To me! To life! May we never be ill again! There he is.

123.   ENTRANCE TO PLAYROOM   STEELE AND AGATHA
Escorted by the housekeeper, he stands at the entrance to the room looking over Judith's gang. We know that he feels slightly alien to this world—not superior to it, just a little uncomfortable. After a moment Alec rushes in to him.

ALEC (after a moment):
> Dr. Steele—do you remember me? Alec Hamm.

STEELE:
> Oh, sure. How are you?

ALEC:
> I'm much better than the last time I saw you, thank you. (Pumps his hand hard.) You did a great job! I knew you could do it! We're all grateful . . .

Dark Victory

COLONEL MANTLE (coming in):
    Dr. Steele, I presume. I've wanted to meet you . . .

124. AT BAR   JUDITH AND ANN
looking off at Steele—Judith rather mischievously. Ann gives her a little push.

ANN:
    Don't be fiendish! Rescue him.

JUDITH:
    Don't rush me.

She goes out.[33]

125. GROUP AT ENTRANCE   STEELE, ALEC, COLONEL MANTLE

COLONEL MANTLE:
    Generally speaking, I regard doctors as a pack of frauds—try to tell me port's bad for my gout!

To Steele's relief, Judith and Ann come in.

JUDITH (as much the hostess as she can manage, but with a twinkle):
    How do you do, Dr. Steele.

STEELE:
    Hello, Judith . . . Ann . . .

JUDITH (to the room in general):
    My friends—this is the gentleman who did my operation . . . Dr. Steele, my gang . . . Now the largish woman with the eagle eye is Carrie Spottswood . . . And this is— Oh, never mind them! Come over here! You're late![34]

Pushes him out.

126. PAN SHOT   TWO
as she drags him toward a comfortable lounge.

STEELE:
I was at the hospital—

JUDITH:
Never mind that. We're not interested in medicine here. Sit down. (Pushes him into lounge.) Have a drink?

STEELE:
No, thanks.

JUDITH:
I had one. You said I could. (Plops down beside him, takes his arm, proceeds lightly.) Thanks for everything again—my drink—my horse—my first day . . .

STEELE (looks at her):
Have you been a good girl?

JUDITH:
No.

STEELE:
I thought not.

JUDITH:
Why?

STEELE:
I knew you wouldn't be . . . I knew you could never be.

JUDITH:
You mean—a good girl? Well—I am!

STEELE:
Did you drive in for lunch and come right back?

JUDITH:
Father, I cannot tell a lie.

STEELE:
What did you do?

Dark Victory

Judith puts up her feet to show him the new shoes she bought.

STEELE:
    Very pretty. What else?

JUDITH (indicates dress):
    This—and other new frocks that will stun[35] you—and thank you so very much for the two inches off my middle . . . (Grows serious.) And thank you for my life. What can I ever do for you? (Thinks of something.) Oh! (Looks around, calls.) Ann!

127.   ANN
    among guests, turns.

128.   FROM HER PERSPECTIVE   JUDITH AND STEELE

JUDITH (mouths silently):
    Has it come?

129.   ANN

ANN (mouths silently):
    I'll see.

goes out of the playroom, CAMERA PANNING.

130.   JUDITH AND STEELE
    He is solemn. She, thinking of the present, is full of anticipatory glee.

JUDITH:
    You just wait! (Turns and sees his solemn face.) Why are you so grumpy?

STEELE:
    You say I'm always grumpy.

JUDITH:
    I've been good until today. Why, I've been your

slave! And I'm well! Look at me! (Crosses her knees, works her reflexes.) Reflexes terrific! (Stands up, puts her feet together.) Balance perfect! (Turns.) And I can walk a line. (Walks one on the floor, CAMERA PANNING.)

131. CLOSE-UP STEELE
Knowing what he knows, this is a dreadful ordeal. We feel that if it goes on, he cannot stand it any longer and will tell her.

132. WIDE ANGLE TWO
with Ann approaching in background.

JUDITH:
Why, I can walk one backward! (Does so for a few steps, then sees Ann, calls to her.) Did it? (Ann motions to her that she'd better go out; Judith turns to Steele.) Excuse me. (To Ann as she goes.) Kneel on him—club him if necessary, but make him have a drink—get that look off his face somehow!

She runs out. Ann watches her proudly, comes to Steele who has risen and has also watched Judith go out.

ANN:
You did that . . . Aren't you proud?

STEELE (overcome with emotion):
I don't want a drink, thanks . . .

He walks out of scene. Ann watches him—perplexed, anxious. She has a premonition that something is wrong. She goes out after him.

133. STEELE AT FRENCH DOORS LEADING TO VERANDA
He opens one of the doors to get some fresh air. Ann comes into scene. She is frightened.

Dark Victory

ANN:
>Dr. Steele—when you came down to Judith's room—right after the operation—you had a certain look in your face . . . I attributed it in my mind to the strain—the tension of the operation.

STEELE:
>I don't understand you.

ANN:
>You have that same look in your face now. I watched you when she was talking to you.

STEELE:
>Miss King,[36] I'd rather—

ANN:
>I'm Irish and I may be psychic and funny. Oh, I might possibly be wrong, but— *Is* there something?

STEELE (with an odd emphasis):
>Something?

ANN:
>Something concerning Judith that—you may be holding back. If there is—please— You see—I *am* her best friend.

STEELE (pause, makes a decision):
>Will you come outside?

They go out.

134.   EXT. VERANDA   ANN AND STEELE come out. She follows him a few steps before he turns to her.

STEELE:
>Are you going to be strong enough and intelligent enough to hear the truth?

ANN:
>There *is* something!

STEELE:
> Yes, there is. I can't save her—nothing can—*nothing.*

ANN:
> You mean she's not—

STEELE:
> Yes. She'll die . . .

ANN (won't take it seriously, doesn't dare):
> So will we all . . .

STEELE:
> She's going to die of that growth for which we operated.

ANN (a sharp cry):
> No!

STEELE:
> It's true.

ANN:
> You shouldn't have touched her!

STEELE:
> I'm not going to argue with you now. The facts are these— I will tell you in simple, layman's language . . .

ANN:
> She'll have that pain again—and that ghastly confusion?

STEELE:
> No. She's not going to suffer again. That's all behind her now . . .

ANN:
> But you told her she could *ride* . . .

STEELE:
> That's the freakish nature of this thing. She will ride

. . . She will seem as well and normal as anyone else.

ANN:
How long have you known?

STEELE:
Since the operation. That night . . . when her fever went to the ceiling—I could have let her go . . . I almost did . . .

ANN:
Why *didn't* you?

STEELE:
I'm only a man. I haven't jurisdiction over life and death.

ANN:
How will it come?

STEELE:
Quietly—peacefully—

ANN:
God's last small mercy! (Pause.) You mean it will come without warning—she'll have no chance to be ready?

STEELE:
There may be a moment very near the end when she won't be able to see quite as usual . . .

ANN:
She'll go blind?

STEELE:
A dimming of vision . . . Then, after a few hours, say two or three . . .

ANN:
Doctor, how long has she? A year? (He doesn't answer.) Six months? Four?

Dark Victory

STEELE:
    Possibly more.

ANN:
    Oh, I don't *believe* it.

STEELE:
    Ann, if I could literally cut off this arm . . .

Ann tries to control her tears. After some time:

ANN (quietly):
    I know.

STEELE:
    Buck up, Ann. She mustn't know. Be a soldier . . .[37]

JUDITH'S VOICE:
    BOO!

and a small package hits Steele squarely in the back.

135.   WIDER ANGLE TO INCLUDE JUDITH
who runs in to them.

JUDITH:
    You sneaks, you're hiding out on me! (She is laughing, but she means it a little, too.) Out here behind my back! What's the idea? (Picks up her package.)

ANN (pulls herself together):
    Actually we were talking about just how much you ought to do. I told him you'd had a devil of a day—and he doesn't seem to think it matters.

JUDITH:
    I've had the best day of my life! (Hands Steele package.) This is for you.

STEELE:
    Judith, you shouldn't . . .

JUDITH:
>   Oh, don't play surprised! You know you doctors always expect your G.P. presents—and if I'm not a grateful patient there never was one.

STEELE (fumbles with package):
>   What's in it?

JUDITH:
>   A little gold and a lot of sentiment . . .[38] Don't open it yet . . .

136.   CLOSER ANGLE   THREE
with Ann watching in the background and wishing she didn't have to. Steele is in torment. Judith looks up at him and for the first time since we have seen her, she is shy.

JUDITH:
>   Do you remember telling me how you happened to become a doctor?

STEELE:
>   You mean that day in the hospital when I ran on so?

JUDITH:
>   Ann, listen— He said that when he was a little boy, the visit of the doctor was always *such* an event. He'd drive up to the house behind a spanking pair of horses—the best in town . . . He'd come in and everyone would make a fuss while he told the latest gossip. You were the patient that time, Fred . . . you had a sore throat . . . Old Doc Smith was the handsomest man in town—wore the best clothes—and he wore those old-fashioned shirts— you know, Ann, with stiff bosoms and stiff detachable cuffs with big gold cuff links. When he took off his coat and shook down his thermometer, his cuff links jangled. This little boy decided right then and there that if he could be a doctor and wear shirts

Dark Victory

like that and have gold cuff links that jangled, he'd want nothing more. (Directly to Steele.) And so you grew up and became the finest doctor in the world . . . (Ann has to turn away.) Now you may look.

Steele is unable to open the package. He stands there with it in his hand, unable to do or say anything.

JUDITH:
Look at the man . . . ! I thought surgeons had to have such steady hands.

ANN (turns back, controls herself):
Let me help you, Doctor.

STEELE:
Thank you.

137. CLOSE SHOT TWO
as together they undo the box. They look at each other—they are comrades, giving strength to each other. The box opened, Steele looks down at

138. INSERT   PAIR OF GOLD CUFF LINKS
with his initials.

139. THE THREE
Braced by Ann, Steele is able to face Judith as if nothing is wrong.

STEELE:
Thank you very much. It's the best present I've ever had.

JUDITH:
I'm so glad you like them. It's all we could think of, wasn't it, Ann? (Starts toward house.) Of course, it doesn't seem enough— (Stops, turns.) Wait! I've an idea! This is my birthday . . .

ANN:
>What?

JUDITH:
>It is—really—my new birthday. Every year on this date we'll meet—just us three pals . . . We'll meet and have a party . . .

ANN (with a strange tone):
>Let's go . . .

JUDITH (thinks it's great fun):
>All right . . . (Goes into playroom.)

A look between Ann and Steele. She takes his arm and they follow her inside. They close the door and CAMERA TRUCKS UP to it. Inside we see the party in progress— Judith very gay, introducing Steele to people. Each of the girls has hold of one of his arms.

>FADE OUT

FADE IN

140. INT. JUDITH'S SITTING ROOM   ANN
is seated at a desk going over a pile of bills and making entries in an account book. She seems to be concentrating, and on her face is a look of worry. We shall come to understand during the course of the next few scenes that this worry has nothing to do with the bills or the accounts but comes rather from a development in Judith's life which really terrifies her. And we shall understand that her concentration on the books is a deliberate attempt at defense against the intrusion of a frightening and tragic subject. At the moment, however, it appears that she is merely busy over her work.

This room connects with Judith's dressing room, and through the open door to this room we hear

JUDITH'S VOICE:
>Now, in the morning I'll wear my green slacks and the small tie— I'll wear the big hat for lunch— He'll

like that . . . I've got to look my best . . . If ever little Judy had to knock them for a row of pins . . .

141. INT. JUDITH'S DRESSING ROOM JUDITH AND MARTHA
are selecting outfits for the weekend. The doors to the wardrobes are open, disclosing quantities of clothes and shoes.

JUDITH:
Now, Martha, it's up to you. Let's see—in the evening— (Calls to Ann.) Ann, do you think we ought to dress for dinner tomorrow night—give him a bit of swish?

142. ANN
barely glances up from her work.

ANN (noncommittally):
Darling, just as you please . . .

143. WIDER ANGLE TWO
as Judith appears at her open dressing room doorway.

JUDITH:
I don't think so— The men will be tired . . . I'm getting to be such a hostess! It's my first real weekend. The house reeks with dignity. Of course we'll have the kids in—I'll always want them—and I don't think he minds them, do you?

144. ANN
listening against her will to Judith's bubbling enthusiasm. She is very agitated.

ANN:
I don't suppose he does.

145. THE TWO

JUDITH (a trifle annoyed):
What's the matter with you, Ann?

ANN:
>Nothing. I've got to get through these bills. It's the tenth of the month.

146–148. OMITTED

149. ANN
>She is desperate and wondering what on earth to do. She puts on a brave front, tries to be gay.

150. PAN SHOT   JUDITH
>goes to Ann.

JUDITH:
>Ann, you'll put on your best dignity, won't you, and help me keep dignified? (Plops on desk before Ann.) Well—I'm here—I think—I'm somewhere very nice . . .

ANN:
>Look at me.

JUDITH:
>I'm looking at you.

ANN:
>You're in love . . .

JUDITH:
>Yes!

ANN:
>Um-hum—I thought so . . . What about him? Has he given you any encouragement?

JUDITH:
>Not a ripple on the water . . . It drives me crazy . . . But when I just think of him, I— When I think that if I hadn't fallen off that horse— Ann, it's awful—but it's wonderful. Life is a different thing. For the first time I get up in the morning with some-

Dark Victory

thing to live for—something besides horses and hats and food. He's very fine, isn't he, Ann? He's worthwhile, isn't he? But, oh, if only the Spaniards or the French had settled New England instead of the Pilgrims—

ANN:
But—if he's given you no sign—how do you know?

JUDITH:
Well—it's just to be hoped for. Time will tell. He's so sweet to me, Ann. And he didn't go away—that's one sign, Mr. Watson . . . Don't be against me.

ANN:
I'm not.

151. WIDER ANGLE
Judith gets off the desk.

JUDITH:
Will you do something for me?

ANN:
Of course.

JUDITH:
I was just thinking that you might take advantage of any lull in the conversation tomorrow—just to mention what a good wife Judith would be—what an ideal wife and mother . . . (Ann doesn't answer.) Well, don't you think I would be?

ANN:
The best.

JUDITH:
Keep both fingers crossed for me. (Going toward bedroom.) One day it'll happen to you, Ann—and then you'll know— It's a grand and glorious feeling!

She goes out and closes the door behind her.

Dark Victory

152. **ANN**
in agony. For a moment or two she tries to think of something—anything to do. She makes up her mind and reaches for the phone.

ANN (into phone):
Get me Murray Hill seven, seven, three, four, zero.

153. **DRESSING ROOM   MARTHA**
hears her call the number.

154. **ANN**
sees Martha in the dressing room, gets up, goes to the dressing room door. As she closes it
DISSOLVE TO:

155. **INT. STEELE'S OFFICE   AT DOOR   ANN**
enters quickly, closes the door.

STEELE'S VOICE:
Come in, Ann.

CAMERA PANS her to him. He has left some papers on his desk to advance to meet her.

ANN:
We have something to talk about.

STEELE:
What's that?

ANN (hesitates a moment):
Is Judith meaning anything more to you—than just—a patient? Perhaps it's impertinent of me to ask . . .

STEELE:
No, it isn't.

ANN:
I think I know. I assume you do care for her.

Dark Victory

STEELE:
Yes. I care—so much.

ANN:
What are you going to do? Are you going out there this weekend and tell her? Take her in your arms? She'll expect you to marry her. Are you? Or is it better for you to go away—leave her to us? Which is better? I haven't slept for two nights . . . And I watched her this morning and—I saw it coming. And just now—a little while ago—I asked her to her face if she cared . . . And she said, "Yes, I do." It's up to you . . .

STEELE:
She said that! You know, Ann, women have never meant anything to me before. I'd never met anyone like her. I was all set—I had plans, arrangements made . . .

ANN:
Yes—Vermont. Why don't you go away—for your own sake—for your work?

STEELE:
Work! When I can't cure her? There's nothing else on my mind. I sit here—I haven't thought of another thing else . . . I'd give my own body . . . ! (A note of frustration.)

ANN (catches her break from him):
Isn't there anything—anything—anything? What has she done that this should happen to her? She's never harmed a soul—never done anything to anyone but kindness . . .

STEELE (goes to desk, picks up letter):
Look, I had a letter from Vienna today—the last finding in the case . . . Here's the translation— Not a chance in the world! I don't know where to look

next . . . (He breaks.) Here's this Heinzig in Vienna—the greatest in the world . . . (Shows her folder containing Judith's case history.) Twelve of them . . . (Ruffles through pages, crumpling them.) "Prognosis negative!" "Prognosis negative!" "Prognosis negative!"

ANN:
Oh, I'm so sorry—for you both. (Steele looks at her; there is a pause.) You couldn't marry her . . . (As he looks at her we see his indecision.) Do you know what marriage would mean to her? A home—children—plans for the future . . . Could you do that to her?

STEELE:
The great thing is for her never to know . . .

ANN:
Could you watch her growing happier every day—with this thing creeping up behind her back? (She breaks.) Could you stand that? *I* couldn't!

STEELE:
It isn't a question of what you or I could stand. The only thing that matters is that she should be happy—every hour . . . (He breaks.)

ANN (almost whispers):
Could it be—a long engagement? [39]

He turns, moves away, comes back, and takes both her hands suddenly.

STEELE:
All my life I've told people what to do . . . Now—Ann, what shall we do?

There is a tap on the door. He looks toward it.

156. WIDER ANGLE   TOWARD DOOR   TO INCLUDE WAINWRIGHT
who enters.

Dark Victory

WAINWRIGHT:
 The telephone, Doctor.

STEELE:
 Thank you. (Into phone.) Dr. Steele, speaking.

157. INT. JUDITH'S BEDROOM   CLOSE SHOT   JUDITH
is at the telephone. Her face is laughing and impish.

JUDITH:
 Are you operating, Doctor? Are you still in your office, Doctor? Could you bring yourself to come down here and have something cold off the ice? There's a very good friend of yours waiting for you here—a grateful patient—Judith Traherne— Case number forty-five— An uneventful recovery . . .

158. INT. STEELE'S OFFICE   STEELE AND ANN
She is watching. He looks off at her and gestures that it is Judith. He almost smiles in spite of himself.

159. INT. JUDITH'S BEDROOM   JUDITH

JUDITH (as before):
 You'd better hurry—I have a vague feeling of relapse. Come on, you Pilgrim pill peddler!⁴⁰

She puts down the receiver, looks around, whistles.

JUDITH (calls):
 Ann!

Goes toward sitting room, CAMERA PANNING.

160. INT. SITTING ROOM
Martha is straightening the room.

JUDITH (coming through door):
 Ann, do you know that man hasn't— (To Martha.) Where's Miss Ann?

137

Dark Victory

MARTHA:
    She's out.

JUDITH:
    Where did she go?

MARTHA (looks at her significantly):
    Didn't you telephone the doctor's office just now?

JUDITH:
    What's that got to do with it?

MARTHA:
    Wasn't she there?

JUDITH:
    No. What do you mean?

MARTHA:
    She telephoned—made an appointment— She said she was coming down. That's where she is. She sees him often.[41]

JUDITH:
    Don't be silly! How do you know?

MARTHA:
    I hear them talking on the telephone. They're talking behind your back all the time. Something goes on between those two.

JUDITH:
    Nonsense! Gossip! I'm sure if Miss Ann is at the doctor's, she must have some very good reason for being there. When he gets here I'm going to have him examine *your* head.

                              DISSOLVE TO:

161.   EXT. DRIVEWAY
Ann's car drives in. She gets out and hurries toward the front door. As she goes through doorway Steele's car drives in behind hers.

Dark Victory

162. INT. LOWER HALLWAY   ANN comes in, starts up the stairs.

    JUDITH'S VOICE (from playroom):
      Ann? (Comes out of playroom.)

    Ann stops on the third or fourth step.

163. ANGLE TOWARD DOORWAY   JUDITH AND ANN IN FOREGROUND
    Judith leans on the stair rail, an intimate, friendly pose.

    JUDITH:
      Where did you go?

    ANN (vaguely):
      For a drive.

    JUDITH:
      Where to?

    ANN:
      To town . . .

    JUDITH:
      What for?

    ANN:
      Oh, I—

    JUDITH (notices Ann's confusion, remembers Martha's words):
      Where did you go?

    This scene is interrupted by the entrance of Steele.

    STEELE:
      Hello . . .

    JUDITH (goes around to him):
      You did hurry.

    STEELE (to Ann, as if he hasn't seen her for days):
      How are you, Ann?

Dark Victory

Without answering, Ann turns and runs up the stairs.

STEELE (watches her):
 Did I stumble into something?

JUDITH:
 Yes . . . (Takes the bit in her teeth.) We were on the verge of a jealous scene about you.

STEELE:
 What?

JUDITH:
 Darling, you poor fool, don't you know I'm in love with you?

Sound off-scene of Ann's door slamming.

164. CLOSE SHOT   STEELE
 looks up in the direction Ann has gone, wondering what has happened, what has been said.

165. CLOSE SHOT   JUDITH
 looking at him, waiting for him to speak. She looks away.

166. BOTH

JUDITH:
 Of course, I've made an idiot of myself . . . But I don't care . . . Naturally, you must be embarrassed . . . You've been proposed to . . . Well, Fred, all you have to say is that you don't want me and—

STEELE:
 Oh, my poor darling.[42]

He gathers her into his arms as one would pick up a hurt child, holds her protectively.

167. CLOSE-UP   JUDITH   OVER HIS SHOULDER
 her great happiness.

168. CLOSE-UP STEELE
his infinite pity.

FADE OUT

FADE IN
169. EXT. STEELE'S BROWNSTONE   JUDITH
has parked her car at the curb and, followed by Terry on a leash, she goes up the steps to the entrance door.

170. CLOSER ANGLE AT DOORWAY   JUDITH
stops and looks at the name on the simple sign beside the door: Frederick Steele, M.D. She cocks her head to one side as she looks at the name and smiles to herself, a warm glow of pride and happiness suffusing her whole being. This name represents so much to her now—not alone the skilled surgeon but her lover, her man, as well—everything great and good. She presses the tip of a gloved finger to her lips and then to his name on the sign as if bestowing a kiss on him. Then she opens the door and she and Terry go inside.[43]

171. INT. STEELE'S WAITING ROOM   JUDITH
comes in with Terry. There is no one else in the room, which is littered with the disorder of packing.

JUDITH:
   Hey! Is anybody home?

172. CONSULTING ROOM   WAINWRIGHT
has her arms loaded with things to pack and is on her way toward the waiting room with them when Judith comes in. Judith lets Terry loose and he investigates the room, sniffing and wagging his tail.

WAINWRIGHT:
   How do you do, Miss Traherne? The doctor's not here.

JUDITH:
   Where is he? I'm to have lunch with him.

WAINWRIGHT:
> He wants you to meet him at the restaurant. I haven't seen you to congratulate you.

JUDITH:
> It's a strange world, isn't it? When I first came here you were packing—and I thought it was the end of my life. Now, you're still packing—but my life is just beginning. Don't stand there with your arms loaded, Wainwright. I'll kill a little time in here.[44]

Wainwright goes out. Left alone, Judith looks about the room. Today she is looking at things with new eyes. She loves the room and everything in it. These things that were his are now theirs. The feels a proprietorship which fills her with pride and happiness.

173. PAN SHOT   JUDITH
She walks around, examining things more closely, touching some of them as she passes.

JUDITH (calls to Wainwright):
> It's nice to marry the man you love. I darn near broke my neck to get him. Of course, it's a perfectly screwy setup . . . Vermont and Long Island . . . We don't live in the same world. Do you suppose Vermont and I will understand each other?

174. WAITING ROOM   WAINWRIGHT
absorbed in her work of packing, paying little attention.

WAINWRIGHT:
> I don't know much about Vermont—except what he's told me.

175. JUDITH
as before.

JUDITH:
> He loves it, doesn't he? Then I will, too. You know,

Dark Victory

> I'm going to sell my house and my apartment—everything—my horses . . . No, I'll keep Challenger— He's a champion. Am I disturbing you?

176. WAINWRIGHT
is very busy.

> WAINWRIGHT:
> Not at all . . .

177. JUDITH
is at a wall straightening a framed certificate of Steele's membership in the College of Surgeons.

> JUDITH:
> I'm glad he's going to give up cutting people open . . . He's one of the great scientists . . . (Walks away, CAMERA PANNING.) And I'll be "Mrs. Pasteur" . . . We'll be useful people in the world.

She sits down at his desk and her manner is amusingly proprietary as she ruffles through the papers that are stacked in some disorder on it.

> JUDITH:
> I'll keep his house and mind his books and answer the mail . . .

The last word of the above speech is read in a slightly altered tone, for among the papers she is handling she has just caught sight of:

178. INSERT   CASE HISTORY FOLDER
labeled Judith Traherne.

179. JUDITH
naturally is interested. She draws the folder toward her, pleased to be able to read something about herself. She opens the cover, sees that the folder contains four or five typewritten pages and also a sheaf of a dozen or more letters held together by a clip. She begins to read the first letter.

180. INSERT LETTER

                KARL HEINZIG
                   Vienna
             September 18, 1938

Frederick Steele, M.D.
Professional Building
New York City
U.S.A.

My Dear Dr. Steele:
    A study of the case history of Miss Judith Traherne and an examination of the tissue samples sent me lead me to concur with your diagnosis. The prognosis is definitely negative.
    Death in such cases is (etc.).

181. JUDITH

stares down at the letter, unable to believe, hardly able to comprehend what she is reading. She finishes the letter, turns to the next. As she reads it she begins to comprehend the dreadful meaning. Terror closes in on her. She quickly glances at the third letter, shuffles through the fourth and fifth. She looks up and around in blind terror, begins to read again.

182. TERRY ON THE COUCH

He looks off at Judith, cocks his head. Sensing something is wrong, he gets off the couch and trots over to her, CAMERA PANNING. He nuzzles against her, but she doesn't notice that he is there. She turns through the last typewritten pages which are her case history.

183. JUDITH

slowly looks up, her world falling to pieces. She must have confirmation. She must be sure. She thinks of Wainwright.

    JUDITH (calls off, making her voice deliberately casual):
        Miss Wainwright . . .

Dark Victory

WAINWRIGHT'S VOICE:
Yes?

JUDITH:
What does "prognosis" mean?

184. WAINWRIGHT
is absorbed in sorting the contents of an office file.

WAINWRIGHT (calls back):
It means what the future of a case looks like.

185. JUDITH

JUDITH:
What does "negative" mean?

186. WAINWRIGHT
busy as before.

WAINWRIGHT:
It means hopelsss.

Suddenly she realizes what she has said—gasps, drops what she has in her hands, rushes into

187. CONSULTING ROOM
Judith is just going out of the door into the corridor, slamming it behind her as Wainwright rushes in. She looks at the door, fearing the worst. She hurries to the desk, looks down and sees what Judith has been reading, looks up aghast.

FADE OUT[45]

FADE IN
188. INT. RESTAURANT JUDITH
alone at a table. The room is intimate and the crowd smart. A small orchestra plays hit tunes from current revues.

A cocktail is before Judith. It is not her first. She looks about at the people, listens to the music.

Dark Victory

(NOTE: Remember in playing the following scenes that the shock Judith has just received is terrific. It is too much for her brain to deal with. It makes her speech disjointed, her look distracted. It is something inside of her, threatening her with hysterics which she forces down. The hysterics never come to the surface. It is a scene played in whispers against music and gay chatter of the smart set at lunch. The scene itself we play down—way down. Make it a ghastly scene the way she plays it.)

189. PAN SHOT STEELE
comes through the room, sits down beside her.

STEELE:
I'm sorry I'm late, darling. I had a consultation. You look lovely.

JUDITH:
Have a drink.

STEELE:
No, thanks.

JUDITH (to waiter):
Another for me. (To Steele.) You should try one some day.

STEELE:
I will . . . Perhaps on our wedding day.

JUDITH:
Our wedding day!

She looks at him and laughs wickedly.

STEELE:
What's the matter?

JUDITH:
Could anything be?

Ann enters scene.

Dark Victory

ANN:
> If I'm late, I'm sorry.

JUDITH:
> Don't be sorry—about anything. Sit down—join the party . . . We're playing games—hide-and-seek—you can play, too—puss-in-the-corner . . .

ANN:
> What are you talking about?

JUDITH:
> I don't know . . . (She watches the two glance at each other.) If you like, I'll leave. You two dear friends probably have a lot to talk over . . . my two dearest friends! Have a cocktail, Ann—I'm going to have another . . .

ANN (quietly):
> Yes, I'll have a cocktail.

JUDITH:
> They're fine . . . They deaden the brain— (To Steele.) You know about brains . . . (Chuckles.) They loosen inhibitions and make the tongue waggle . . . You should both have one.

ANN (with a smile):
> Are you quite well?

JUDITH (with irony):
> You should know how well I am. (To Steele.) Am I well? (To both.) Ssh . . . it's a secret! Or wouldn't you know about secrets?

CARRIE'S VOICE (off-scene):
> Judith, darling!

190. ANOTHER ANGLE
as Carrie comes in to Judith. Judith turns to her, as she nods to the others.

Dark Victory

JUDITH:
> Carrie, dear—what a nice hat. You remember the eminent Dr. Steele . . .

Steele rises.

CARRIE:
> Of course . . . (Offers hand to Steele.) Judith tells me you're frightfully good. Would you look me over sometime? I've been feeling a pain—

JUDITH:
> Oh, my dear, if you've anything wrong with you, anything at all—fly to him at once!

CARRIE:
> I will. (To Judith.) Will I see you at the Radcliffe Hunt next week?

JUDITH:
> Of course.

ANN:
> Darling, aren't you forgetting that you're going to Vermont?

JUDITH:
> Oh, yes, Vermont. (To Steele.) I hear it's cold in Vermont.

STEELE (making conversation):
> In the winter—but it's nice.

JUDITH (inwardly shuddering):
> Yes, it will be winter—with the ground cold under the snow . . .[46] (Gaily; to Carrie.) You must come to Vermont, Carrie.

CARRIE (uneasy at having run into what is apparently a situation; with a prop smile):
> Yes. Well, anyway, it was nice seeing you, dear. Good-bye, Ann. Good-bye, Doctor . . . (Escapes.)

Dark Victory

JUDITH (as Carrie goes and Steele sits down):
    I've meant to ask you, Doctor . . . Was I a specimen case? Will I make the medical journal?

ANN (distracted):
    Shall we order? Waiter . . .

STEELE:
    Why don't you tell me what this is all about?

JUDITH:
    Why don't you tell me? Why *didn't* you tell me? (Takes menu from waiter.) I think I'll have a large order of prognosis negative.

ANN (frightened):
    What do you mean?

JUDITH:
    You know . . . Oeufs sur le plat . . . *prognosis negative!* (While Ann and Steele look at each other in shocked amazement; then she gets up; to Steele.) Do you know what prognosis negative means, Doctor . . . ? Explain to her—or have you . . . ? A few months of pretending you're well, then blindness, then— (Starts away.) So long, my *friends!*

191.   ANOTHER ANGLE
They follow her, catch her.

ANN:
    Wait, Judith! We can't talk here but—

JUDITH (interrupting):
    Oh, yes we can! It was a question of humor the patient. Pet her. Give the poor darling everything she wants. The time's so short—marry her if necessary! Now I know why you went to his office that day— It was to beg him to marry me—out of pity. You're both so kind—thank you very much.[47]

Dark Victory

STEELE:
>Judith—you're wrong— (Catches her arm.)

JUDITH (cringing):
>Don't touch me, please. (Starts away.)

ANN (catches her):
>Judith, what else on earth could we have done?

JUDITH:
>You could have told me the truth—I can take it.

Goes swiftly out, CAMERA PANNING.

192. ANN AND STEELE
stare after her.

FADE OUT[48]

FADE IN

193. INT. NIGHTCLUB   MIRROR SHOT OVER BAR TO SHOW SECTION OF ROOM

There is nothing special about the place. It's just a tiredly gay night spot—thick tobacco smoke, a few customers. It is near closing time.

Plainly shown is an orchestra. The conductor is a violinist, and a girl in evening clothes works with them. They are midway through a number, "Oh! Give Me Time for Tenderness," which the orchestra is playing to dance tempo. Some of the customers are dancing. The girl is singing. Her lyrics are:

>Let my heart be still and listen to one song of love,
>Let me feel the thrill of quiet we know nothing of.
>Oh! Give me time for tenderness
>To hold your hand—and understand
>Oh! Give me time.

194. THE ORCHESTRA
The music stops and the boys in the orchestra begin to pack up for the night. The CAMERA FLASHES OVER on a PAN to Judith and Alec at the bar. Her head is averted.

Dark Victory

She is looking at the orchestra. A tired barman moves in to them.

BARMAN:
   It's two o'clock. Last drink, sir.

Alec is drunk almost to the point of weaving.

ALEC:
   Three here and three here—same thing.

Judith turns. She is drunk, too, but she doesn't know it, and at first we do not realize it. She is frozen with drunkenness. Her expression is set—only her lips move. There is a wild look frozen in her eyes.

JUDITH:
   That's funny—

ALEC:
   What?

JUDITH:
   Time, Alec . . . Did you ever think about time? It goes, Alec—that's the business of time—Tick, tick, tick—you can almost hear it go by. Before you know it, it's all gone by and then where are we, my friend?

ALEC:
   We're high and dry—that's the last drink.

Judith looks back at the orchestra and there is a mechanical quality to her movement that tells us she is drunk.

JUDITH:
   I want that song again.

ALEC:
   What song?

JUDITH:
   That song she was singing about time.

Dark Victory

    ALEC (looks off toward orchestra):
        Too late again.

195.   ORCHESTRA
    packing up to go.

196.   PAN SHOT   JUDITH
    leaves the bar, comes to the orchestra—to the girl.

    JUDITH:
        You wouldn't mind singing that song once more, would you?

    GIRL:
        Sorry—it's bedtime . . .

    JUDITH (fishes in her purse):
        You mustn't go to bed. Mustn't sleep. It's a great waste. Time doesn't sleep. That's a joke. Here— (Hands her fifty-dollar bill.)

197.   GIRL AND ORCHESTRA LEADER
    They exchange a significant look. They think they've got a mad woman on their hands—but fifty dollars is fifty dollars.

198.   ANOTHER ANGLE   JUDITH AND GROUP
    The pianist sits at the piano and begins to run over the opening chords of the number. Judith hands another fifty dollars to one of the orchestra men.

    JUDITH:
        Play . . . Sing and play . . .

    She picks up copy of the song in order to follow the lyrics.

199.   CLOSE-UP   PIANIST'S HANDS
    beginning the song. PAN to the girl singing.

Dark Victory

199A. OTHER ANGLES
as the boys of the orchestra unpack their instruments and join in one by one.

199B. LONG SHOT
Some of the customers think another dance is starting and get up on the floor to dance.

199C. SIDE ANGLE   JUDITH AND GIRL
Judith is leaning in the curve of the piano. The girl is singing to the customers, with her back almost to Judith. Occasionally on pertinent lines, Judith just glances down at the song. The complete lyrics:

> Oh! Give Me Time for Tenderness
> I will never ask for more than you can give,
> Yet when you say, "Be gay today and live,"
> My heart answers cautiously, "Today will soon be gone,"
> Why rush to meet our destiny?
> Why must we hurry on?
>
> REFRAIN:
> Oh! Give me time for tenderness,
> One little hour from each big day,
> Oh! Give me time—to stop and bless
> The golden sunset of a summer day.
> Let my heart be still and listen to one song of love,
> Let me feel the thrill of quiet we know nothing of,
> Oh! Give me time for tenderness,
> To hold your hand—and understand,
> Oh! Give me time.
>
> © 1939 Warner Bros. Inc. Copyright renewed. All rights reserved.

199D. CLOSE MOVING SHOT
As the song finishes the CAMERA MOVES AROUND to a BIG CLOSE-UP of Judith—"Oh! Give me time." The look in her eyes frightens us.[49]

FADE OUT

FADE IN

200. INT. RIDING CLUB BUILDING   CORRIDOR LEADING OFF JUMPING RING   CLOSE SHOT   A TABLE
on which is arranged a display of cups.[50] From off-scene we hear the sound of applause from a large audience.

201. WIDER ANGLE   CORRIDOR
There is a cluster of people about the entrance to the ring, from which point they have been watching the show inside. They, too, are applauding. Judith appears from the riding ring. She is in riding clothes, has just ridden.

SOMEONE:
   Nice work, Judy.

JUDITH (touch of irony):
   Hurrah for me.

As she crosses corridor to door to dressing room Carrie falls in with her.

CARRIE:
   You were wonderful, dear . . . In spite of it all, you still retain your seat . . .

202. INT. DRESSING ROOM   PAN SHOT   JUDITH AND CARRIE
come in, go toward dressing tables. Carrie is being a cat. Her manner is *too* sweet.

CARRIE:
   I don't know how you do it. It amazes me you can stick on a horse . . .

They reach Judith's dressing table. Martha is there with a suitcase in which there are evening things.

JUDITH:
   Hello, Martha. How's everything at the old homestead?

MARTHA:
   All right, Miss Judith.

CARRIE:
> Of course, I'm your dear friend and I don't care *what* people say about you . . .

JUDITH:
> Nice of you.

Martha has helped her off with her coat and she sits down.

CARRIE:
> Take *all* their husbands and sweethearts—drink the town dry—I'd still say it's none of my business—but—

JUDITH (pointedly):
> And I'd agree with you.

CARRIE (in a huff):
> Well, of course, if you want to adopt *that* attitude. You can already fill the Yale Bowl with people who are sore at you. One more won't matter.

JUDITH:
> Martha, I don't think I can change without a drink.

WIPE OFF TO:

203. INT. BAR ADJOINING RIDING RING   FULL SHOT
There are quite a number of people in the room, coming to and fro, etc. At the bar there is a group of the lads of the town, including Alec. Standing a little apart from this group, his hat in hand, is Michael, looking at the entrance. He sees Judith come in. She is dressed now in a particularly sleek evening outfit.

JUDITH:
> Hello, Michael.

204. CLOSER ANGLE   TWO

MICHAEL:
> I've got the horses packed. I put chains on the cars—it's snowing outside. You did very well.

JUDITH:
> Thanks. What's the matter with you?.

MICHAEL:
> I waited to see you . . . I wondered if you'd care to drive back with me. That mare's got bronchitis and can't possibly last the night.

JUDITH:
> Jessica's Girl?

MICHAEL:
> Yes.

JUDITH (carelessly):
> Why don't you put her out of her misery? I'll get there if I can.

She walks to the group at the bar, CAMERA PANNING.

JUDITH (to group at bar):
> There's a tragedy for you! (Laughs; there is a quality of cruelty in her laughter.) Jessica's Girl has bronchitis and can't possibly last the night. Jessica's Girl is a horse! Poor Jessica's Girl!

205. MICHAEL
gives her a look, half resentful, half perplexed, goes out.

206. GROUP AT BAR
Judith climbs upon a stool.

JUDITH (to bartender):
> The usual.

ALEC (with amused resignation):
> Here we go again.

An anxious little man, a minor official of the horse show, comes in to Judith.

ANXIOUS LITTLE MAN:
> Miss Traherne—if you don't mind—they want you to come—the presentation of the cup . . .

JUDITH:
  Oh, yes, the cup—the darling cup . . . (To group.) Excuse me, kids, I've won a prize.

She leaves the group and, CAMERA TRUCKING AHEAD of her, goes out of the room. The anxious little man accompanies her part way, then with a hasty

ANXIOUS LITTLE MAN:
  I'll tell them you're coming.

he hurries on ahead. Judith's progress takes her into a wide corridor (or a clubroom) which connects the bar with the horse show arena. Apparently this place is deserted, but Judith suddenly stops as she looks up and sees

207. **STEELE**
  waiting for her. He walks toward her.

208. **THE TWO**
  as Steele comes to her. She has dreaded this meeting with him, but all the time knowing it was inevitable. Now that it's here, she rises to it with cold defiance.

JUDITH:
  Well, if it isn't the extraordinary surgeon . . .

STEELE:
  I've tried to see you . . .

JUDITH:
  How's your mortality rate these days, Doctor? Any more fun with the knives?

STEELE:
  Drop it, Judith.

JUDITH:
  Why aren't you in Vermont with the bugs?

STEELE:
  You know why I'm not. I want to talk to you.

JUDITH:
> When I need a doctor, I'll send for one. I'm not in your care any longer.

STEELE:
> You'll always be in my care.

JUDITH:
> Will I? Is that part of your duty—to hang on until the very end and watch through those scientific eyes—

STEELE (seizes her roughly):
> *Drop it!*

She just looks at him, then slowly and coldly extricates herself from his grasp.

STEELE:
> I know how you feel—anything to strike back at me. But don't do it this way . . .

JUDITH:
> What do you mean—this way?

STEELE (with a gesture):
> This . . . There's nothing in it.

JUDITH:
> What do you want me to do—sit alone in my room and think how in a few months—

STEELE:
> Judith, I want you to find peace. We all have to die. The tragic difference is that you know when and we don't. The important thing is the same for all of us—to live our lives so we can meet death—when it comes—decently—beautifully—finely.

JUDITH:
> Finely . . . beautifully . . . I'll die as I please. Leave me alone!

STEELE:
> Do you hate me so much?

JUDITH:
> Oh, so much and for so many reasons. I hate you for not telling me the truth. I hate you for letting me hurl myself at your head. Oh, I'm so *ashamed!*

STEELE (pause):
> I can understand.

She gives him a little quick look.

209. WIDER ANGLE
as the anxious little man reappears.

ANXIOUS LITTLE MAN:
> Miss Traherne—please—They're waiting!

JUDITH:
> Let them wait. *They've* got plenty of time . . . Oh, all right.

She starts out.

210. BAR   TWO MEN
drinking, and looking off at Judith.

FIRST MAN:
> There she goes. She's riding high.

SECOND MAN:
> Traherne? She's on the town.[51]

A hand reaches in and pulls him around abruptly.

210A. WIDER ANGLE   PAST THE MEN TOWARD ALEC
who is standing next to them at the bar. Steele enters scene behind Alec.

ALEC:
> You happen to be talking about a very good friend of mine.

Dark Victory

SECOND MAN:
> You too, Alec? She's a friend of all the lads.[52]

Alec makes a move to hit him, but the man is faster and knocks Alec down. Then, almost immediately, he himself is on his back, as Steele smashes him. Steele looks at the man's companion as much as to ask if he'd like some of the same thing. But apparently he wouldn't. Then Steele walks back to Alec and helps him to his feet.

STEELE:
> Shall we leave, Alec? There's an odor of gentlemen around this club.

He and Alec start away, CAMERA PANNING. They pass Carrie.

CARRIE:
> I wish I knew Judith's prescription. Men never fight over me. I've never stirred up so much as a dog fight.

> > > > > > > > FADE OUT

FADE IN

211. INT. STABLES   CLOSE SHOT   SMALL SIGN on stall: Jessica's Girl. CAMERA PULLS BACK. A vet is stooped over a horse who is down on the straw—the horse being suggested rather than seen. Michael stands nearby, and Spec, with a lantern. In the background we see Judith approaching, walking toward the stalls through the dim lights and shadows. A long fur coat hangs carelessly from her shoulders.

VET (looks at thermometer):
> Respiration's easier. She'll pull through. (To Michael.) Nice work. Lucky we got it in time.

Judith reaches the stall. She looks down at the horse. They all watch her. There is a long pause.

JUDITH:
> Well? Is she dead?

Dark Victory

MICHAEL:
> No. It was touch and go for a while. It's more touch than go now. (Wipes sweat from forehead.) Whew! I actually said a prayer. She's game. She put up a brave fight.

JUDITH:
> How nice.

Turns and walks away. Michael follows her.

212.   PAN SHOT TWO
Michael catches her, walks beside her. He is in a happy mood now the horse is out of danger.

MICHAEL:
> Can I take you home?

JUDITH:
> No, thanks. I've a car.

MICHAEL:
> Got your chains? It's pretty heavy going.

Judith opens the stable door. A strong wind blows snow in at her.

JUDITH:
> It's snowing.

MICHAEL:
> Yes, the old year's dying out. (Judith shivers.) You're cold. (Pause.) There's a stove in the feed room. I've been sitting in there off and on tonight. Would you like to come and warm yourself?

JUDITH (considers for some time before answering):
> Why not?

She walks past CAMERA toward the feed room. Michael watches her a moment, and without looking toward the stall, says:

MICHAEL:
> Spec! (Spec hurries in, carrying the lantern. Michael takes it from him.) You can go to bed.

Spec scuttles away without a word. Michael follows Judith. In the lantern light we see his eyes—excitement in them.

> WIPE OFF TO:

213. INT. FEED ROOM
The room is in darkness except for the glow from the stove and the light cast by the approaching lantern.

Judith and Michael appear. In the lantern light we see the room dimly outlined—the stove, a rough desk and chair, the grain bins, the piles of straw.

Without saying anything, Judith walks to the stove and warms her hands over it. Michael comes to the desk in foreground and sets the lantern on it.

MICHAEL:
> The first cold's always the bitterest.

JUDITH:
> The first and the last . . . (To drive away these thoughts.) Talk to me, Michael.

Michael goes to her. CAMERA MOVES UP with him.

MICHAEL:
> What shall I talk about, Miss Judith?

JUDITH:
> Anything. Just talk.

MICHAEL:
> It was a great show tonight. I came to think you may not be entirely wrong about Challenger.

JUDITH:
> Thank you very much.

MICHAEL:
> I was scared though.

JUDITH:
> Was I that bad?

MICHAEL:
> No, but there's something about the way you ride that puts my heart in my mouth. Can I say something to you, Miss Judith?

JUDITH:
> Go ahead. I told you to talk.

MICHAEL:
> You've been going too hard, Miss Judith . . . Night and day . . . You can't do that and keep on with your jumping horses. It's terrible hard on you. I was hoping that in the state you were in, you wouldn't ride tonight. A silver cup isn't worth it.

CAMERA PANS with Judith as she walks over to a pile of straw.

JUDITH:
> I wanted that cup. (Sinks down wearily on the straw.)[53] I had to show the gentry that I still have what it takes.

214. MICHAEL
looks off at her.

MICHAEL:
> You sure have.

215. JUDITH
gives him a quick look. There is a dead pause. Then,

JUDITH:
> I told you to keep on talking.

She leans back against the straw.

216. BOTH
as he walks toward her.

MICHAEL:
> You know, you and I are kind of alike.

JUDITH:
> Are we? How?

MICHAEL:
> You've got the spirit in you the same as I have in me. It's the fighting that counts. You've got to have action in your life just like I've got to have action in mine . . . We only live once, Miss Judith.

JUDITH:
> Just once— (Breaks away from thoughts.) Tell me about you, Michael.

MICHAEL (laughs):
> Me?

JUDITH:
> Keep on talking—just as one human being to another. It's always been about the horses.

MICHAEL:
> What's there to say?

JUDITH:
> Do you have a happy life, Michael?

MICHAEL:
> Not always. I've thoughts I have to smother down.[54]

JUDITH:
> Thoughts? What thoughts?

MICHAEL:
> I guess I was born out of my time, Miss Judith. I should have lived in the days when it counted to be a man—the way I like to ride and the way I like to fight. What good's riding and fighting and having good muscles these days? What do they get you?

Dark Victory

217. **JUDITH**
    takes out cigarette and lighter.

    JUDITH:
    What do you want?

218. **MICHAEL**
    looks at her.

    MICHAEL:
    I told you I have thoughts to smother down.

219. **JUDITH**
    looks up at him. She lights the lighter. The light shines in her face.[55]

220. **MICHAEL**
    springs out of scene.

221. **BOTH**
    Michael snatches the lighter from her hand.

    MICHAEL:
    Are you trying to burn us up?

    JUDITH:
    Are you afraid to burn, Michael? Are you afraid to die?

    MICHAEL:
    I wouldn't want to die—while you're alive . . .

    JUDITH (pause):
    You're making love to me . . .

    MICHAEL:
    You invited me talk to you as a man, and it's as a man I'm talking . . . Surely I'm better than some of them that's playing around with you. They're afraid of you. I've heard them talking. They'd go after you, but they're afraid. I wish that I was in their boots!

JUDITH:
> Do you, Michael?

MICHAEL (takes her in his arms):
> You wouldn't need to risk your lovely neck jumping horses for excitement. The nights I've laid awake thinking of you . . . The things I've wanted to say to you ever since the first time I saw you . . .[56]

JUDITH:
> Say them, Michael . . .

MICHAEL:
> We're of a kind. Will you belong to me and no one else?

He kisses her. For a moment she doesn't care. Then she pulls away.

JUDITH:
> No, no . . . Let me go, Michael.

MICHAEL:
> You're afraid.

JUDITH:
> No—but—

MICHAEL:
> So I'm only a stable hand, am I?

JUDITH:
> It isn't that . . . I can't go on this way. Tonight it would be you and after tonight, what?[57] You again—or someone else—and so on and on until the last hour. Michael, I can't die like that . . .

MICHAEL:
> Die? What's this crazy talk about dying?

JUDITH:
> I'm going to die in a few months, Michael. (He lets

go of her and stares down at her.) Does that frighten you?

MICHAEL:
Heaven forgive you for saying a thing like that. (Stares at her, shocked and incredulous.)

JUDITH:
Yes, heaven forgive me. When it comes, it's got to be met finely—beautifully—doesn't it? (She breaks completely.) I'm all shot, Michael.

She collapses onto the straw.[58]

DISSOLVE TO:

222. INT. JUDITH'S BEDROOM JUDITH
comes slowly in. We see that her bed is turned down and her nightie laid across it. There is a light by the bed, but otherwise the room is in darkness. She goes to the bed and sits wearily on it. She is tired—very tired. The wild passions of hate and bitterness and excitement have calmed, leaving her in the awful empty mood in which she finished the scene with Michael when she said, "I'm all shot, Michael."

She picks up the telephone. When in the following scene she speaks, her voice is empty and dead.

JUDITH (into telephone, wearily):
Murray Hill seven, seven, three, four, zero, please.

ANN'S VOICE (from sitting room):
Is that you, Judith?

JUDITH:
Yes, Ann.

She listens to the phone ringing at the other end of her call as Ann comes through from the sitting room. Ann wears her sleeping pajamas (or nightie), slippers, and robe. She has been waiting up for Judith, and we realize that she has done it many times—and always has greeted her without any resentment or pique—just as she greets her now. But we see that the strain of the past weeks has been very great on Ann. She is near the breaking point. It takes an effort for her to speak and act normally.

ANN:
It's very late. I was afraid something had happened.

JUDITH:
No . . . You should be asleep, Ann. Poor Ann, you've lost a lot of sleep.

ANN:
Where did you go after you left the club?

JUDITH:
To the stables. I've been with Michael.

ANN:
Judith!

JUDITH:
Don't worry, Ann. I was saved. Of course, for what I was saved is not quite clear. (Hangs up the phone.)

ANN (almost breaks, chokes it back):
Whom were you calling?

JUDITH:
It doesn't matter. There wasn't any answer. Business of apologizing to a gentleman for ruining his life along with mine. But I don't suppose it matters. (Sinks back on bed.) Oh, Ann, I'm tired—tired . . .

ANN (she is gripping herself to keep from hysteria):
Let me put you to bed.

JUDITH:
Why?

ANN:
I'll read you to sleep.

Dark Victory

JUDITH:
    Why? So I can dream?

ANN (breaking):
    Judith, don't talk like that! Please don't, Judith—

JUDITH:
    It's the waiting, Ann—day and night . . . Ann, would it be wrong if I made it happen? Would it?

ANN (breaks, sobbing on the bed):
    Judith—Judith, darling, please don't—

JUDITH:
    What shall I do? What can I do? What would you do?

                                    DISSOLVE TO:

223. INT. ALEC'S APARTMENT LIVING ROOM   NEAR MORNING
ALEC AND STEELE

Steele is sitting in a chair, smoking a pipe. Alec is pacing up and down with an empty highball glass in his hand. He goes to a table on which there is a half-empty whiskey bottle and another half-empty glass.

ALEC:
    Have another drink? (Pours himself a drink.)

STEELE:
    No, thanks . . .

ALEC (begins to pace again):
    I love that girl, Steele, with every atom of my down-at-the-heel soul. When I see her like this—What the devil's wrong with her?

STEELE:
    I can't tell you.

ALEC:
    I know it's something between you two. You were the man—the one big thing . . . We all had our money on you.[59] (Sound of doorbell. He goes to door.) Don't let it get you down.

224.　　AT DOOR　ALEC
opens it to reveal Judith. She is still wearing her evening clothes and her fur wrap. She is somewhat disheveled. In her manner she wears a pathetic mask of gallantry to hide her weariness and hopelessness.

JUDITH:
　　Hello, Alec.

ALEC:
　　Hello.

She walks in.

225.　　WIDER ANGLE TO INCLUDE STEELE
who has risen.

JUDITH:
　　Hello, Doctor . . . Look here, I'm sorry . . . This is a fine time to be out, isn't it? I hope you're not operating today.

STEELE:
　　No, I'm not.

JUDITH:
　　I searched half the town for you two. I even rang the doctors' night bell. I thought doctors were always on twenty-four-hour duty.

ALEC (brightly):
　　Would you kids like an egg and bacon? The dawn is well up.

JUDITH:
　　No, thanks . . . Yes.

ALEC:
　　I just thought of it as a way to get me out. I'm bright that way. (Goes toward kitchen.) Pour yourself a drink, Judy.

He goes out.

226.   MED. SHOT   STEELE

He picks up the bottle of Scotch, which is on the table near the sofa, and is about to pour a drink when she comes in.

STEELE:
   Shall I?

Judith shakes her head. He sets down the bottle.

JUDITH:
   Can you ever forgive me?

STEELE:
   There's nothing to forgive.

JUDITH:
   The things I said to you!

STEELE:
   It's good to say things. It gets them out. I do understand.

JUDITH:
   Do you? Can you? You said you wanted me to have peace. Where is peace?

STEELE:
   Within yourself.

JUDITH:
   I've tried to do the things I said I would, tried to carry through to the last empty boast. Tonight— Darling, there's been no one but you. How good it is to call you that. I had to come to tell you—no one. I couldn't go on with you bitter toward me. Please don't think of me like that. (She is breaking.)

STEELE:
   I love you, Judith.

JUDITH:
   Yes. I believe you. It isn't just pity. I take back every unkind thing I said to you. Fred, help me. I've been

Dark Victory

so stupid. I've crammed every minute so full of—waste. Now there's so little time. I don't know what to do. I'm afraid! You're so great and right and strong—

She breaks down completely, sinks to her knees on the floor and, burying her face in the sofa, sobs. The tears come in a great flood. The dam has burst. It is a relief to be able to cry like this. During all of it she hasn't once cried before.

He goes over and sits beside her, puts his hand on her head very gently.

227. CLOSE SHOT TWO
Her sobs die out.

STEELE:
It's all right now, Judith.

JUDITH:
If only you'll let me see you sometimes . . .

STEELE:
You're going to—every day. I'll show you what peace I can. You're coming with me to Vermont.

JUDITH (looks up):
Am I? (For a moment her face lights up; then.) No. It wouldn't be fair to you. We'd only have—

STEELE (silencing her):
Forever. Will you marry me, Judith?

The sun is up and shines on her face as she looks up at him.

JUDITH:
Marry? Wouldn't it be marvelous if we could—a real wedding . . . given away . . . church bells and champagne . . . a white frock, orange blossoms, and a wedding cake . . . That's one thing I won't

Dark Victory

have missed—and you're giving it to me. I can never love you enough.

FADE OUT

FADE IN

228. EXT. STEELE'S VERMONT FARMHOUSE LONG SHOT DAY
The season is winter, probably January. The sky is dotted here and there with heavy clouds which herald the imminent arrival of snow. The bare trees are whipped by a biting cold wind.

We see Steele's farmhouse, a very old New England wooden structure that belongs to the landscape. Near it is the one-story wooden structure—probably formerly the cookhouse—which he has converted into a laboratory. From the chimneys of both these buildings smoke pours, attesting to the warm fires within.

As the scene FADES IN we see a very old country mailman, bundled into heavy clothing against the cold, making his way up to the mailbox before the house.

WIPE OFF TO:

229. EXT. BACK OF FARMHOUSE AT KITCHEN DOOR
Judith, followed by Terry, comes through scene, reading letter. They go into kitchen.

230. INT. KITCHEN JUDITH AND MARTHA
Martha is working in the kitchen, possibly preparing vegetables. Judith, followed by Terry, comes in, looks up from the letter.

JUDITH:
A letter from Ann!

MARTHA:
Is she coming up?

JUDITH:
Not yet . . . soon, I think . . . (Reads from letter.) "Still trying to rent the house—but no one seems to have any money and I'm not going to let tramps

Dark Victory

have it . . ." (To Martha.) Why do people complicate their lives so? All those horses—that house . . . Here we have nothing—and yet we have everything. (Reads from letter.) "Enjoyed the snapshots . . . I saw the lawyer about those bequests—and everything will be as you wish . . ." [60] (Mumbles on.)

231. MARTHA
looks at her. From the fact that she is not shocked we realize that she understands and is in the pact that they make no mention of death in this house.

MARTHA:
I wonder that she hasn't popped up to see you . . . You haven't seen her for three months.

232. JUDITH
A little look that shows she and Ann have discussed this and understand each other.

JUDITH:
Oh, she'll be up . . . She said she wanted to get the work done . . . What's that? A baked potato? Hasn't he had his lunch yet?

233. BOTH
as Judith goes to the stove.

MARTHA:
I knocked at his door—twice. (Opens warming oven.) Then I fixed a tray and knocked again. When he's busy with his bugs, he's like a bear with a sore head. I wouldn't disturb him . . .

JUDITH:
I'll disturb him! (Gets tray; at door.) Am I afraid?

She goes out in a high mood.

234. EXT. FARMYARD   JUDITH
crosses quickly and with determination from the house to the laboratory. Goes in.

235. INT. LABORATORY PREPARATION ROOM   JUDITH
bursts through on her way to the second room.

236. INT. CULTURE ROOM [61]   STEELE AND ASSISTANT
Steele is bent over his black cloth-covered worktable cutting a cell culture for transplantation. The assistant stands by with tools. Judith bursts in.

JUDITH:
   Hey!

STEELE (looks up, aghast):
   Judith! I've told you—

JUDITH:
   You were rude to Martha.

STEELE:
   I was not rude to Martha. Martha knows—as you should know— (To assistant.) Oh, well, the damage is done.

JUDITH:
   What damage? Me?

This is a comedy row that they carry on almost continuously. They are always acting with each other, living at a high pitch to ignore the situation.

STEELE:
   I've told you never to come in here when I'm working. This joint is aseptic. You're crawling with microbes.

JUDITH:
   A fine way to talk about your wife!

STEELE (sees tray; to assistant):
> Will you take that food out of here? We've got too many bugs in here now . . . (To Judith.) You come bursting in here with microbes just when I was discovering the secret of life . . . (Catches assistant's eye and recovers his humor.) Well . . . I'm not so sure we were this minute.

JUDITH (contrite):
> Yes, but you will. You would have now, but— It's my fault.

STEELE (takes her in his arms):
> Forget it. My little bugs have met your little bugs and the food's little bugs—and they're going to have a party—and they'll get so cockeyed drunk they'll be of no use to anybody . . . (To assistant as he returns.) Take 'em outside and set up another dish. If at first you don't succeed . . . Come along, honey . . .

Takes her out into

237.   PREPARATION ROOM   PAN SHOT   JUDITH AND STEELE
come through.

STEELE:
> Say, I'm hungry! (Accusingly.) Do you know it's almost two o'clock?

He starts for the tray of food that the assistant just put on the table.

JUDITH:
> Don't touch that—it's probably got some of your bugs in it. If the sandwiches' bugs got into your bugs, it's not improbable that your bugs got into the sandwiches'.

Takes him out to

238.   YARD   PAN SHOT   JUDITH AND STEELE
go to kitchen.

>   STEELE:
>   What's new in the world?
>
>   JUDITH:
>   Guess what? Ann's coming soon. Look.

Hands him the letter. He reads it during:

>   STEELE:
>   What did you do this morning?
>
>   JUDITH:
>   Big things . . .
>
>   STEELE:
>   What?
>
>   JUDITH:
>   I walked.

They go into

239.   INT. KITCHEN   JUDITH, STEELE, MARTHA, TERRY

>   STEELE (as they come in; is still reading letter):
>   Where did you walk?

Martha begins dishing his lunch. Terry comes to Steele and gets a pat.

>   JUDITH:
>   The village . . . (To Martha.) Can we sit at your table?
>
>   MARTHA:
>   What if I said no?[62]

By now his lunch is on the kitchen table. Steele folds up Ann's letter, places it in the envelope, makes no mention of its serious contents.

STEELE:
> This is great. We'll give the old girl a field day. We'll show her the great village of Brattleboro . . . We'll show her the city hall . . . We'll drive her down the boulevards . . . (Terry pokes his nose up and Steele gives him a scrap of food from his plate.) We'll show her the shopping district . . . and we'll take her to the dance on Saturday night! (Turns back to find Judith has picked up fork and is about to take a bite from his plate.)[63] Hey!

DISSOLVE TO:

240. INT. STEELE'S CAR JUDITH, ANN, AND STEELE (PROCESS BACKGROUND)

(NOTE: Car drives through the village, out toward the countryside. If a PROCESS SHOT for the background proves difficult, put a lot of frost on the windows.)

Steele is driving, Ann beside him, Judith on the outside. Ann's baggage is piled in the back seat. We must remember this is the first time in months that Ann has seen Judith. In a way she has dreaded this meeting, apprehensive of the mood she might find between these two. To her intense surprise she finds this gay, high mood they sustain between them. She has expected to be sincere and sober, but they won't allow her to. Gradually—toward the ene of the scene—she is swept into their mood and becomes one with them. As they drive along, Judith turns suddenly and, for no reason at all, gives Ann a terrific hug.

JUDITH:
> Oh, it's grand to see you!

ANN:
> You said that.

JUDITH:
> Well, I say it again!

Ann is self-conscious. She looks out of the wide window.

Dark Victory

ANN:
    So this is New England?

JUDITH:
    Yes.

ANN:
    It's beautiful, isn't it?

They look out the window and there is silence for a moment.

JUDITH (sees someone on the street):
    Freddy, it's Mrs. Adams. (Calls out the window.) How's the sciatica?

241. ANN AND STEELE
A quick look between them, her perplexity, his reassurance.

242. ALL THREE
as Judith turns back.

STEELE:
    What did she say?

JUDITH:
    I don't know. But I suppose she's all right. She's walking.

There is another pause. Judith looks at Ann. She can't give her another squeeze, but she wants to break the silence.

JUDITH:
    How's Long Island?

ANN:
    The same as ever . . .

JUDITH:
    Did you let the house?

ANN:
> Yes.

We feel the driving force of Judith. She is taking control of Ann, not Ann of her. With death at hand, she is in supreme command of the situation.

JUDITH:
> What else? Michael . . . ?

ANN:
> Cheeky as ever. The new tenants have taken him on.

JUDITH:
> And how's the horse who dances on the lawn? How's my Nemesis?

ANN:
> Michael says he's wintering well.

JUDITH:
> So are we . . . I want to tell you, darling, you'll need your flannel underwear in this burg. Have you got them on?

ANN (smiles):
> It is a bit nippy . . .[64]

· DISSOLVE TO:

243.   EXT. FARMHOUSE   JUDITH, ANN, STEELE, AND MARTHA
The three get out of the car, still laughing. Martha is waiting for them.

ANN:
> Martha! How are you?

MARTHA:
> I'm first rate. It's good to see you, Miss Ann. (Looks her over.) You're looking a bit peaked.

JUDITH:
> We'll fatten her up—a little country gravy—

Dark Victory

ANN (looks over the house):
    It's perfect. (Points off to lab.) What's that?

STEELE (has been getting bags out of the car):
    That's my laboratory. Come on . . . (Takes her out.)

JUDITH (calls after them):
    Don't let her in—she's got bugs, too! (Turns to Martha.) Let's unpack for her, hm?

244. ANN AND STEELE
come in from outside.

ANN:
    Oh, it's very attractive.

He takes her across room, CAMERA PANNING, opens door to second room to let her look inside during:

STEELE:
    She fixed it over . . . Used to be the old cookhouse. Of course here's where the real work goes on. We can't go in.

ANN (looks inside second room):
    It looks marvelously efficient. (Turns to him anxiously.) How's the work coming actually?

STEELE:
    So-so . . . Up one blind alley, down another. Someday—in our time—in some other time—

ANN:
    Fred, is there a chance for her?

STEELE:
    No.

ANN:
    Oh, I'd so hoped . . . And then when I saw her . . .

STEELE (distressed):
> Don't hope. (Shuts door, a gesture of emphasis.)

ANN:
> But all this . . .

STEELE:
> May save others—someday. That's all, Ann, I can't make an appointment for a miracle to happen!

Ann puts her hand on his arm, a gesture of understanding and comfort. She herself is near tears. There is a pause.

ANN:
> Does—Judy fully realize . . .

STEELE:
> Yes.

ANN:
> Oh, I can't believe it. She couldn't bear it. No one could. Secretly, she must believe—

STEELE:
> All my life I've seen people suffer and seen them die—but I've never seen anyone like her. From what deep well she draws her courage, I can only wonder. I'd have cracked without her. She's beyond words. You saw her. She laughs and sticks out her chin. She can take it.

ANN:
> She can't always. No one could. There must be bad moments—when she thinks—

STEELE:
> She doesn't think. It's forgotten. That's our pact. We never mention it. You mustn't either. You'll want to. But you mustn't. Not even with your eyes.

ANN:
> Fred, I couldn't—

STEELE (sharply):
   You're in the pact, too.

ANN (pause):
   I'll try.⁶⁵

FADE OUT

FADE IN

245. EXT. STEELE'S FARMHOUSE   SIDE ANGLE
PAST ENTRANCE TOWARD ROAD
The snow has melted. The trees have young leaves. Young plants are pushing their way through the earth in the flower beds. It is early spring.

Beside the house in the foreground Ann is taking packages of seeds out of a parcel recently arrived. She is in a gardening outfit and wears gloves. Tools lie about on the ground. As she takes each package out she looks at it, reading the names to herself. Michael and Judith come out of the house.

MICHAEL (calling back):
   So long, Doc.

JUDITH:
   Don't say "Doc." It isn't respectful.

ANN (calls to Judith, holding up package):
   Here's a tongue twister. Incomparabilis.

JUDITH (correcting her pronunciation):
   Incomparabilis. Plant them where there's plenty of sun.

ANN (other packages):
   Jonquilla . . . Narcissus . . . What a pretty name—Jonquilla Narcissus!

MICHAEL:
   I'll name a horse after it.

ANN:
   Go along with you.

MICHAEL:
    So long, Ann.

246.   TRUCKING SHOT   JUDITH AND MICHAEL
TAKING THEM to his car in the roadway. We should also see Steele's car in the driveway.

MICHAEL:
    Say, about the Grand National . . . A thousand dollars is a lot of money to waste.

JUDITH:
    It isn't wasted. I'll bet you six to four that Challenger wins.

MICHAEL:
    Taken.

JUDITH:
    You know, Michael, I'm actually excited about going to Philadelphia! I'm going to wear my best clothes and go on a tear.

MICHAEL:
    Can I drive you down?

They have reached his car.

JUDITH:
    No, thanks.

MICHAEL:
    When I look at you now—well, it makes me believe in those prayers I've been saying.

JUDITH:
    Ssh, Michael . . . (Pushes him into car.) Run along. I'll see you at the National . . . If we can't make it for any reason—think of me.[66] Good-bye . . .

She hurries back down the hill toward Ann.

Dark Victory

247. **REVERSE ANGLE   PAST ANN TO JUDITH**

    JUDITH:
      Ann, do you notice how dark it's getting? He'd better take his overcoat. It isn't spring yet.[67]

248. **ANN**

    ANN (in surprise):
      Why, Judith—

    She looks up at

249. **SKY**
    with the sun blazing down.

250. **PAN SHOT   JUDITH**
    coming toward her.

    JUDITH:
      It's getting darker by the second. Why, how dark it's gotten.

251. **CLOSE-UP   ANN**
    Chills of terror come over her.

252. **THE TWO**
    Judith has not yet seen Ann's face. She is looking down at her hands, which she holds out in front of her, slowly turning them in the sunlight.

    JUDITH:
      It's funny I can still feel the heat of the sun.

    She looks up at Ann.

253. **ANN**
    is looking at her. She looks away, trying to hide her face, for she knows what it is showing.

254. CLOSE-UP   JUDITH
as she comprehends. Her hand flies quickly to her throat and there is a sharp intake of breath.

JUDITH:
Agh! (Terror.) Ann!

255. BOTH
as Ann flies to her and they throw their arms around each other. They cling together in terror and Ann is wracked with dry, frightened sobs.

256. CLOSE-UP   JUDITH   OVER ANN'S SHOULDER
as she very slowly gains mastery over her fear and in the inevitability of the truth becomes calm.

ANN (gone completely to pieces):
No, it isn't true! There *are* clouds— The sun *has* gone!

JUDITH (comforting her):
It's all right, Ann . . . Ann—it's all right . . .

STEELE'S VOICE (from house):
If the Ladies' Gardening Group can adjourn their meeting for a moment . . .

257. STEELE   IN UPPER WINDOW

STEELE (continuing):
I've got some news. We're not going to Philadelphia. We're going to the big burg. We're going to New York.

258. SIDE ANGLE   GROUP   PAST THE GIRLS TOWARD HIM

STEELE:
They just read me a wire over the phone. Come in, I'll show you.

He disappears from the window. Judith and Ann look at

each other. The fact that it's New York, not Philadelphia, means nothing, but it does remind them of the expected journey.

ANN:
    Judith, you can't—

JUDITH:
    Don't tell him . . . Maybe it isn't anything . . . Come on—

She goes out toward house. Ann follows.

259. INT. HALLWAY   STEELE, JUDITH, AND ANN
He comes bounding down the stairs, a paper in his hand, as Judith and Ann come in from the garden.

STEELE:
    This is great news!

JUDITH:
    What's happened?

STEELE:
    Read that! A wire from Fisher in Philadelphia. Martha took it down.

He shoves the paper into her hand, waits, bursting with pride, for her to read it. Ann is staring at Judith with a white, drawn face. Judith looks down at the paper.

260. INSERT   PAPER
as seen by Judith. The paper is dark. The message is in blurred writing which she cannot read.

261. CLOSE SHOT   JUDITH
is looking down at the message, taking a great deal of time about it, wishing she could read it, wondering how she can pretend that she has.

STEELE'S VOICE (impatiently):
    Well?

JUDITH (looks up; a little smile):
   How nice.

262.   WIDER ANGLE   THE THREE

STEELE:
   How *nice!* Is that all?

JUDITH (quickly to Ann):
   Read it, Ann. I never could read Martha's writing.

She flashes her a quick look of anguished appeal.

STEELE:
   Of all the profound understatements . . .

Ann, understanding Judith's predicament, has taken the paper and begins quickly to read.

ANN:
   "Dr. Frederick Steele, Brattleboro, Vermont: Wild with excitement over your latest report. Biological tests convince me you may be on right road with isolation—"

STEELE (cuts in):
   Isolation, see? Choke off the oxygen. No, you two wouldn't understand . . .

ANN (continues reading):
   "Believe we should present material at board meeting in New York tomorrow. Please wire. My enthusiastic congratulations. Fisher."

JUDITH:
   It's wonderful, darling. Isn't it, Ann? Please excuse what seemed my lack of enthusiasm. I was—bowled over for a minute.

STEELE:
   Sure! Don't I know? I'm in the clouds myself. I wired Fisher I'd meet him at ten in the morning.

JUDITH (he's leaving!):
  Oh, did you?

STEELE:
  It means driving to Mills Junction to catch the four forty. Come on. (Starts upstairs, CAMERA PANNING.) Martha's packed you, but I can't even find my socks.

263. JUDITH AND ANN
  Ann starts to speak—to stop him!

  JUDITH (quickly, quietly):
    No.

  ANN (looks at her, aghast):
    What are you going to do?

  JUDITH (confused):
    I don't know . . . Nothing . . .

  ANN:
    You can't go.

  JUDITH:
    No . . .

  ANN:
    Well, you can't let him go!

264. STEELE FROM THEIR PERSPECTIVE
  comes out of the bedroom to landing.

  STEELE:
    Say, I'd gladly stay with you and help plant those bulbs . . . I wouldn't even mind being late except that this board convenes just twice a year. Some of the men are coming from Boston—some even as far as Kansas City. And a very distinguished man—Heinzig of Vienna—is coming. And those men are going to sit around that table and tell if your little boy is right or not. Shake a leg, honey. (Hurriedly goes back into bedroom.)

Dark Victory

265. JUDITH AND ANN

JUDITH:
Would you want me to stop that?

ANN:
Judith, you can't send him away without knowing . . . I won't—

JUDITH:
Ann—please go out and go on with the flowers as if nothing has happened . . . Dear Ann . . . please . . . I know what's best.

She goes up the stairway, CAMERA PANNING.

266. ANN
watches Judith go up. She doesn't know what to do. With a dry sob, she turns and goes out the front door.

267. INT. BEDROOM
It is a nice room, cut into odd shapes by the roof, furnished in chintz, a four-poster bed.

Steele is struggling with his packing. Judith's bags are packed and waiting. On the bed two of her traveling outfits are laid out, a gray and a black.

STEELE (yells):
Judith . . .

JUDITH'S VOICE:
Coming.

STEELE:
You know what this means, don't you—if it's true. It means that in ten—fifteen—twenty-five years, I'll begin to get someplace.

Judith comes in.

JUDITH:
It's very exciting, isn't it?

Dark Victory

STEELE:
I'll say it is. Maybe we'll be acclaimed. Maybe we'll get our pictures in the paper. (Points to outfits on bed.) Say, which of those do you want to wear—the gray or the black?

JUDITH:
I'm not going, dear.

STEELE (astonished):
What?

JUDITH (any excuse to avoid looking at him; to keep it casual):
Look! You've not packed enough shirts. (Goes to dresser.)

STEELE (follows her):
Come out of it, Judy.

JUDITH:
I'd rather not . . . You'll be busy . . . I'd just be sitting around in a hotel room . . .

STEELE:
Nonsense. A couple of days in New York will do you good. You can buy some new clothes.

JUDITH:
I don't need any new clothes.

STEELE:
You can see your friends . . .

JUDITH:
Please, darling, don't force me to go.

STEELE:
Force you . . . ? Well, of course, darling, it's anything you want, but—

JUDITH:
New York would bore me, really it would. This is my home now. I'd rather stay here.

In packing the shirts, their hands come in contact.

STEELE:
> You're trembling!

JUDITH (this is a dangerous moment):
> Am I? Well, it's the first time we've been separated. Mayn't a girl get a little sentimental?

STEELE:
> Judith, I'm not going.

JUDITH:
> You must.

STEELE:
> I don't know what I could have been thinking about. I'll call Fisher and tell him . . . (Starts out.)

JUDITH (knows how she can stop him):
> Darling—are you worried about me?

Steele stops suddenly, turns. Here it is—the moment they have tried to avoid all the time they have been together. His face becomes grave.

STEELE:
> Every minute you're not in my sight.

JUDITH (smiles):
> You needn't be . . . Ann's here . . .

Goes on packing. She has to keep busy.

STEELE:
> Yes. But if anything should happen . . .

JUDITH:
> It won't. But even so—I'm not afraid anymore.

STEELE:
> Judith, we agreed—

JUDITH:
> That we wouldn't talk about it? Yes, I know. (Holds

Dark Victory

up pair of socks.) Look, a hole! Wouldn't you make a fine picture at that board meeting with your big toe sticking out!

He doesn't laugh. He goes to the bed and sits on it.

JUDITH (goes on packing):
    I used to be afraid. I died a thousand times. The next time death will come as an old friend—gently—quietly . . .

STEELE:
    Oh, my God, Judith!

JUDITH:
    We've had so much . . .

STEELE:
    Just minutes!

JUDITH:
    If we lived to be a hundred, we could have no more. I've been so happy. When the time comes—

STEELE:
    When it comes, I'll go with you.

JUDITH:
    Fred!

STEELE:
    I swear I will!

JUDITH (this brings her to him):
    No, you won't. You couldn't be that unkind to me.

STEELE:
    Unkind?

JUDITH (sits down beside him):
    You see, my darling—you've done so much for me—you've given me the bravery I needed. Do you understand how much that's going to mean to me? Mayn't I—in return—know that I've given you the bravery to go on living?

STEELE:
>I couldn't live without you.

JUDITH:
>You must. You must go on with your work.[68] (Gets up.) Come on. Help me with this. (Goes to suitcase, starts to strap it.) Help me, Fred!

Tries to strap the suitcase. He comes and helps her with it.

JUDITH:
>I wouldn't want my death to be futile and meaningless . . .

STEELE:
>It is! Futile—meaningless—cruel—

JUDITH:
>No. Not if you take revenge for it.

STEELE:
>Revenge?

JUDITH:
>Revenge! By wiping out this thing that is going to take me away from you. (Hands him suitcase.) You must . . . You will . . . (Emphasizes her words by pushing him out of the room.) And with each blow you strike, you'll say, "That was for Judith—my wife!"

268. UPPER HALLWAY AND LANDING   PAN SHOT   JUDITH AND STEELE
come out, go toward landing.

JUDITH:
>Now, no more nonsense. You run along to New York and have your big moment—and I'll wait home as a proper wife should. (Pause.) Have I been a good wife, Fred?

They stop on landing before window. He turns to her.

STEELE:
> Oh, my dear!

JUDITH (smiles):
> That makes me very happy—happier than anything else. I've loved it so—every minute. How can I make you understand? Look out there . . . (Points out window.)

269. CLOSE-UP TWO
looking out the window.

JUDITH:
> Somehow, it's been like that—shining and quiet.

STEELE:
> Judith, I can't lose you.

JUDITH:
> You'll never lose me. Nothing can hurt us now, for what we've had can never be destroyed. That's our victory—our victory over the dark. And it's a victory because we're not afraid.

There is a long pause as they look into each other's eyes. His tenseness relaxes and he smiles.

STEELE:
> Thank you, Judith.

JUDITH:
> You must hurry now . . . (Takes him out.)

270. STAIRWAY
as they come down. Her impulse is to brighten the mood now, to send him away gaily.

271. PAN SHOT TWO
as she brings him down to the foot of the stairs. She is very gay now. She gets his overcoat and hat from the banisters, hands him the coat, puts his hat on his head.

JUDITH:
> Tie your tie properly and brush your hair . . . (Starts him toward door.) And for heaven's sake, buy a new hat.

STEELE:
> This is a good hat.

JUDITH:
> I don't want you going before all those men looking like a country farmer.

272. EXT. HOUSE AND GARDEN
Judith and Steele come out to Ann, who has been planting the flowers.

JUDITH:
> Come and say good-bye to the old boy, Ann. He's off.

273. ANN
realizes that Judith really means to send him away. She looks at Judith, meaning to protest.

274. JUDITH
stops her with a look.

275. WIDER ANGLE THREE
as Ann joins them.

STEELE (takes paper from pocket):
> I had made a list of the places we could be reached . . .

JUDITH (takes it quickly):
> We won't need it.

STEELE:
> Always best to have things in order. So long, Ann. Take care of everything.

ANN:
>I will.

JUDITH:
>Hurry, dear . . . you've got to drive like mad.

STEELE (goes to Judith):
>Good-bye, darling.

They kiss. Judith makes no attempt to cling to him, does nothing that might give the show away.

JUDITH:
>Mind yourself in the big city.

She turns him around and gives him a little push toward the car.

276. WIDER ANGLE   TOWARD CAR   THE THREE
Steele hurries to the car. He throws the bag in the back seat, turns.

STEELE:
>I'm going to be awfully lonely.

JUDITH:
>Don't tempt me. Get going.

He gets into the car and starts off.

277. CLOSE   JUDITH
watching him.

JUDITH (calls):
>Hurry home.

278. STEELE   IN CAR
As he turns out of the lane into the roadway he waves.

279. JUDITH AND ANN
Judith waves back. Ann has turned away. Judith watches the car drive down the road. Then she goes to

Ann and takes the slip of paper that Steele has left, tears it into little bits, and drops them on the ground.

ANN:
> Judith!

JUDITH (calmly):
> Have you planted the hyacinths yet?

ANN:
> Yes . . . no . . . I don't know . . .[69]

280. TRUCKING SHOT TWO

as Judith takes Ann to the flower bed. She holds on to Ann. She is walking as if she can't see very well.

JUDITH:
> I'd like to help you with them. They're his favorite flowers.

Ann, fighting for control of herself, stoops down among the packages and locates the hyacinth seeds.

ANN:
> Here they are.

JUDITH:
> I'm afraid I won't be much help, but if you'll dig the holes, I can drop in the seeds.

ANN:
> Darling, you shouldn't—

JUDITH:
> Please, Ann. I want to very much.

Ann does as she has been asked. With a small planting trowel she digs holes in the soft earth and Judith drops in seeds during:

JUDITH:
> They should do very well in this soil. The garden will be very beautiful in June with everything

blooming . . . I can see it. You will take care of my flowers, won't you . . . you'll water them well . . .

ANN (barely able to speak):
Yes . . .

JUDITH (after a moment):
And Ann—will you take care of my doctor? Will you? Do you know what I mean, Ann?

ANN:
Judith, please!

JUDITH:
He'll need someone. He mustn't be alone. It's so much worse for him than me. (Ann breaks.) That's really true. I'm the lucky one. All I'll miss is growing old—being sick and tired and worn out. Promise me you'll never leave him.

ANN:
I promise.

JUDITH:
Don't cry, Ann. I'm very happy, really I am. (Pause.) Now let me see—I think that's all . . . No, there's one more thing. When Michael runs Challenger in the Grand National—I'm sorry I won't be there to see him win—he will—you must be sure to have the box decorated with my colors. And I'd like my friends there—Alec, if he's back from Europe, Colonel Mantle—anyone else you care to have. Give them champagne—make it a party . . . I'd like them all to be as happy as I am. (Gets up.) I think I'll go in now.

Ann gets up and takes her hand. They walk toward the house, CAMERA GOING WITH THEM.

JUDITH:
I walked to the old mill this morning. It's very beautiful with the new leaves on the trees. Why don't you walk down there and watch the sun set?

Dark Victory

ANN:
>Do you think I'd leave you?

JUDITH:
>Please understand . . . No one must be here—no one. I have to prove to him that I can do it alone. Maybe it will help him over some bad moments in the future to remember it. Be my best friend, Ann. Go *now!*

With a sob, Ann runs away. CAMERA PANS with her as she runs toward fields.

281.   JUDITH
goes toward the house. As she is almost blind now, she has to feel her way up the steps to the front porch. She goes inside.

282.   INT. LIVING ROOM   JUDITH
comes in, goes to his desk, tidies it, handling his personal belongings lovingly. Terry, who has been snoozing in the doctor's big leather chair, gets down and goes to her. Judith feels him against her leg, reaches down, and pats him. Terry whimpers.

JUDITH:
>Watch over him, Terry.

Then she goes back into the hallway. Terry follows.[70]

283.   INT. HALLWAY   JUDITH
comes out of living room, hears noise from kitchen.

JUDITH (calls):
>Martha . . .

MARTHA (appears from kitchen):
>What is it, Miss Judith?

JUDITH:
>I'm going to lie down for a while. I don't want to be disturbed.

Dark Victory

She makes a show of walking up the stairway rapidly and straight. Martha watches her. Terry follows Judith.

284. LANDING JUDITH
stops and for a moment looks out the window. Then she goes on toward the bedroom. Occasionally she touches the wall to make sure of her bearings. Terry follows her. She finds the bedroom door and they go inside.

285. INT. BEDROOM SHOT
Judith and Terry come in. She goes to the windows and pulls the blinds. Then she goes to the bed and lies down. She is reaching down to pull up the comforter when Martha comes in, goes to her.

286. CLOSER ANGLE TWO AT BED
Martha helps her with the comforter.

MARTHA:
 Are you all right, my child?

JUDITH:
 Oh, *yes*, Martha.

287. CLOSE-UP MARTHA
looks down at her with such a look that we realize all of a sudden that she knows everything, but she says nothing, turns, and leaves the room and closes the door.

288. CLOSE SHOT JUDITH
reaches over and gets the doctor's pillow and hugs it to her. She smiles.

289. TERRY LYING ON THE FLOOR
watching her with his head on his paws.[71]

FADE OUT

FADE IN

290. EXT. BELMONT RACE TRACK   CLOSE SHOT   BUGLER
(STOCK)   DAY
blows the call to the post. (Blend this into music, which continues to end.)

                                                            DISSOLVE TO:

291. LONG SHOT   (STOCK)
The track, the stands jammed with people, noise and gaiety. The horses come out.

                                                            DISSOLVE TO:

292. ON TRACK   MED. SHOT   THE HORSES   (STOCK)
go by, one by one in a line, magnificent thoroughbreds. CAMERA HOLDS to let each one pass through until we PICK UP No. 5, Challenger. CAMERA MOVES ALONG with him. He is in fine shape. His coat shines. His withers glisten with perspiration. He looks about and tosses his head impatiently.

                                                            DISSOLVE TO:

293. INSERT   PROGRAM

MATTED DOWN TO:

NO. 5   CHALLENGER
Bl. c. 4   By Victory—Field Nurse
Owner: Estate of Mrs. Frederick Steele
Trainer: M. O'Leary

                                                            DISSOLVE TO:

294. THE STARTING GATE   (STOCK)
They're off!

295. THE CROWD   (STOCK)
up with a roar.

                                                            DISSOLVE TO:

296. THE HORSES AT A JUMP   (STOCK)
go over in a bunch.

                                                            DISSOLVE TO:

Dark Victory

297. ANOTHER JUMP (STOCK)
 perhaps a spill. CAMERA PANS with the horses. Challenger begins to pull away from the field.

   DISSOLVE INTO:

298. ANOTHER JUMP (STOCK)
 a really tough one. Challenger in and over. CAMERA PANS BACK TO SHOW the field far in the rear.

299. THE CROWD (STOCK)
 roaring

300. A BOX CARRIE AND OTHERS

   CARRIE:
   Number five . . . Isn't that Judy's horse?

   A GIRL:
   Judy?

   CARRIE:
   You remember Judith Traherne . . .

   THE GIRL:
   Oh, yes . . . The girl who married her doctor . . . She's dead, isn't she?

   CARRIE:
   Now, hang it all, why didn't I make a bet on him— for luck.

   CAMERA PANS AWAY TO:

301. JUDITH'S BOX
   CAMERA MOVES UP. The box is decorated with Judith's racing colors. In the box are Alec and Colonel Mantle in front, Ann and Steele behind them.

   ALEC (puts down field glasses; to Colonel):
   He's just galloping, Colonel!

   COLONEL MANTLE (watching through glasses):
   If only he doesn't fold up in the stretch.

Dark Victory

    ANN:
        He won't!

    Steele looks away, grief for Judith sweeping over him.

302.   CLOSER ANGLE   ANN AND STEELE

    ANN (looks at him with great sympathy):
        Fred . . .

    STEELE:
        I can't take it, Ann.

    ANN:
        She'd want you to . . . To see her colors carried to the front. (Speaks off.) Colonel Mantle, is there anything more beautiful to watch than courage?

303.   CHALLENGER   (STOCK)
    running

304.   CLOSE SHOT   HIS HEAD   (STOCK)
    the true head of a thoroughbred.

305.   LONG SHOT   (STOCK)
    With Challenger thundering down toward the finish, lengths in front.

306.   AT FINISH LINE   A GROUP OF TRAINERS
    watching the horses come down the stretch. We hear the sound of their hooves. One of the trainers moves aside and we see Michael. Tears are streaming down his tough face.

    A TRAINER (to Michael, but watching horses):
        You've got it, O'Leary, you lucky stiff. A long shot like that.

307.   CHALLENGER   IN THE WINNER'S CIRCLE
    with a horseshoe of flowers around his neck. Michael is hugging the horse.

Dark Victory

MICHAEL (intensely emotional):
　　She could have told them . . . She knew . . . It's in the breeding. If only the little lady could have been here to see it.

　　　　　　　　　　　　　　　　DISSOLVE TO:

308.　JUDITH'S BOX　ANN AND STEELE
Ann has been looking down at Challenger in the winner's circle. She looks at Steele. He is looking down at the floor. Seeing this race, Challenger winning, this reminder of Judith, has been torture. (Change music to "Give Me Time for Tenderness.") Ann puts her hand on his arm.

ANN (gently and quietly):
　　Fred, I think we'd better be going. I promised Dr. Fisher you'd meet him at five o'clock. (Steele barely shakes his head.) He's understood. He's been patient. Your work can't stop now. We can't let her courage have stood for nothing.

He slowly looks up at her. She looks back at him steadily. After a moment the grief drops away from his face and he looks up and beyond her.

STEELE (nods):
　　All right.

　　　　　　　　　　　　　　WHIP CAMERA UP TO:

309.　TREETOPS AGAINST THE SKY [72]

　　　　　　　　　　　　　　　　　　FADE OUT

THE END

Notes to the Screenplay

Apart from the ending, which Warners deleted before *Dark Victory* went into nationwide release in the spring of 1939, the screenplay is a fairly accurate guide to the film. A comparison with the dialogue transcript reveals an increased effort on the part of Robinson (and probably on the part of Goulding as well) to prevent anything from obscuring the film's focal point, which was Judith's victory over death. During filming lines were reassigned, roles were pared, and characterizations altered. Alec's part was reduced, Michael's interest in Judith was underplayed until the stables scene, and Martha went from a Margaret Hamilton type to a sympathetic housekeeper. Lines that would give Judith the aura of a saint or a martyr were deleted.

1. The film opens differently. The first shot is of Michael calling the Traherne house from the feed room and waking up Agatha, Lucy, and Ann, who appear in that order. During the credits one hears only the Resignation theme, not the sound of a telephone. It is interesting that Robinson wanted to begin on a note of such immediacy.
2. Agatha speaks this line in the film since the housekeeper would be more likely to pick up the phone first. Agatha's "Who is it, Lucy?" becomes Lucy's "Who is it, Agatha?"
3. Dissolve to Judith's bedroom. The first shot of Judith is prefigurative: her eyes are closed.
4. In the film the Irish setter's name is Daffy; Judith also has another setter, Don. Most of the dialogue in scene 11 is not in the film, nor are scenes 12–16.
5. Line omitted in film along with reference to fender.
6. Scenes 19 and 20 are not in the film.
7. In the film Michael does not allude to Judith's beauty. Robinson apparently felt it was too soon for him to admit he was attracted to her.
8. In the film the line is almost a put-down: "Oh, but darling, you have the character. You're always telling me so yourself."
9. In the film Judith speaks the line, which is more appropriate.
10. Really a wipe.

Notes to Pages 67–113

11 The second sentence ("When . . . counts") is omitted in the film. After Michael's next line, wipe to Judith on Challenger.
12 Scene 29 is not in the film. One can see Alec's role being pared to the bone.
13 The substance of scenes 30–38 was transferred to the screen except that Judith has a moment of double vision (shown by optical printing) before she steers Challenger into the jump. Scene 39 is not in the film.
14 Scene 44 is not in the film.
15 In the film Steele refers to Judith as a "Long Island nitwit."
16 An unmistakable allusion to George Gershwin (1898–1937), who died of a brain tumor.
17 Scene 47 is not in the film.
18 Changed to the more accurate "sensory nerves."
19 Judith's outburst does not occur in the film, and Steele's speech continues through "Would you mind removing your coat, please?" Since Judith is wearing a coat-dress, her response ("Well, I'm afraid this coat is all there is") embarrasses Steele, who settles for pushing up her sleeve.
20 Since Steele does not test Judith's vision in the film, this part of the examination is never shown.
21 In the film Steele makes his decision immediately: "Cancel the tickets."
22 Line omitted in film, probably because of its bluntness.
23 Glioma is a tumor originating in the central nervous system. Most gliomas are malignant. Thomas J. Fahey, Jr., M.D., has conjectured that Judith's was a glioblastoma multiforme, an extremely malignant tumor almost invariably found in the cerebral hemispheres.
24 In the film scene 76 ends here.
25 Fade in on plaque of Fairview Hospital with off-screen voice of Judith refusing to wear hospital gown ("I said no and I mean no").
26 Scenes 83–93 are not in film, further evidence of the reduction of Alec's role.
27 Just a simple fade out.
28 The doctors' ad libs in this scene (and in the next one) are not in film.
29 Scene 99 is not in film; Alec is not present during the operation.
30 Dr. Parsons is also in scene 100.
31 Fade in on insert of Judith's discharge paper ("Complete surgical

recovery. To be discharged today") juxtaposed with an invitation from "your grateful patient" to a cocktail party.
32 Michael does not say this in the film; he cannot be so familiar. Remaining dialogue in scene omitted.
33 Scene 124 is not in film.
34 This speech is not in the film. Judith is remarkably subdued; her gratitude to Steele gives her restraint.
35 "Stun" was too flighty; Judith is demure in the scene. In the film she speaks of "other new frocks I think you'll like."
36 Having called her Ann, Steele cannot be so formal as to say "Miss King."
37 Fortunately this line was cut.
38 Judith's next line is "Look at the man" in scene 136. All the dialogue in between is omitted.
39 Line omitted in film. The suggestion was so macabre it could provoke laughter.
40 Another deleted line that, although said in jest, would not fit the new Judith.
41 In the film Martha does not speak this line, and the rest of the conversation is omitted because it is so petty. Martha is not a gossip, nor is Judith a jealous woman.
42 The exchange would have been out of character. In the film Judith simply says, "Darling! Poor fool! Don't you know I'm in love with you?" as the Blindness motif is heard. Embarrassed by her admission, she asks Steele if he would like some tea and then adds, "Sorry." Steele replies, "You couldn't have said anything I wanted to hear more. Judy, dear, I love you so much." Fade out on their embrace.
43 Scenes 169 and 170 are not in the film, nor does Judith enter Steele's office with her dog.
44 Line deleted; "killing time" is not especially subtle under the circumstances.
45 It is a wipe, not a fade.
46 Line deleted presumably because it was too portentous.
47 It is here that Judith says, "So long, my friends," and exits. The remaining dialogue is not in the film; it would have been anticlimactic.
48 Again a wipe, not a fade.
49 After scene 197 the camera focuses on Judith listening to the song. Without the activity described in the screenplay, from scene 198 to this point, the episode has a poignant simplicity.

50 The scene really fades in on an insert of a program for the Long Island Hunt and Horse Club horse show.
51 The two lines become one: "Judy's certainly on this town, all right." The fight starts because "on the town" has overtones of dissipation and promiscuity.
52 Line deleted along with remaining dialogue. There is a wipe to the stable (scene 211), not a fade.
53 Judith does not sink down on the straw. *The Outlaw* (1943) was still several years away.
54 This line and the next are not in film.
55 Scenes 217 and 218 are not in film. In 219 Judith uses a match, not a lighter. Her tossing the match on the floor prompts Michael's response in 221.
56 The next three lines are not in the film. Robinson tried to prune the scene of romantic excess.
57 In the film the line is less blatant: "First it's this, then something else."
58 Nothing so theatrical. Wipe to Judith going up the stairs to her bedroom.
59 The line became "You're the one man so be nice to her, will you?" Reagan put the stress on "man," giving the line a connotation he later regretted.
60 Deleted. A reference to lawyers and bequests would automatically evoke death, which would not be the right mood at this point.
61 In an earlier draft, Robinson, always the realist, noted in a parenthesis that he had obtained a "technically correct description" of such a laboratory.
62 Line deleted. Martha is never sassy. In the film she says, "Why, of course, Miss Judith."
63 The business is different in the film. Judith burns her fingers in the oven, and Steele kisses each hand.
64 Scenes 240–242 are not in film; Ann simply arrives.
65 Scene 244 is much shorter in film. Steele merely tells Ann to act as if nothing will happen. There are no references to any pact.
66 Line deleted. Judith is not yet thinking of death.
67 In the film the line is powerfully simple: "Ann, there's a storm coming."
68 Judith's next three lines are not in the film, nor does she ask Steele to help her with the suitcase. She is trying to conceal the fact that she cannot see. When Steele says "futile—meaningless—cruel," it is in response to her line, "You must go on with your work."

69 Wipe to Ann leading Judith to flower bed and another wipe to the two of them planting the hyacinths.
70 Scene 282 is not in film.
71 Scenes 283–289 appear differently on the screen. Judith starts climbing the stairs, stopping midway to call down to her dogs, Daffy and Don, who run up for their last embrace. She makes her way to the bedroom, and when Martha enters, she is kneeling in prayer. Judith climbs up on the bed, and Martha covers her with a comforter. There is no dog by the bed. "I don't want to be disturbed" is the final line of both Judith and the film. Judith's face appears in close-up and then goes out of focus. The End.
72 The Grand National (scenes 290–309) originally ended the film, but after a preview, Warners deleted it because it was clearly anticlimactic. It would also have made the film a "weepie."

Production Credits

Executive Producer	Hal B. Wallis
Associate Producer	David Lewis
Directed by	Edmund Goulding
Screenplay by	Casey Robinson
From the play by	George Emerson Brewer, Jr., and Bertram Bloch
Music by	Max Steiner
Photography by	Ernie Haller, A.S.C.
Film Editor	William Holmes
Sound by	Robert B. Lee
Art Director	Robert Haas
Gowns by	Orry-Kelly
Orchestrated arrangements by	Hugo Friedhofer
Musical Director	Leo F. Forbstein

Released: April 1939
Running time: 106 minutes

Cast

Judith Traherne	Bette Davis
Dr. Frederick Steele	George Brent
Michael O'Leary	Humphrey Bogart
Ann King	Geraldine Fitzgerald
Alec	Ronald Reagan
Dr. Parsons	Henry Travers
Carrie	Cora Witherspoon
Miss Wainwright	Dorothy Peterson
Martha	Virginia Brissac
Colonel Mantle	Charles Richman
Dr. Carter	Herbert Rawlinson
Dr. Driscoll	Leonard Mudie
Miss Dodd	Fay Helm
Lucy	Lottie Williams

Inventory

The following materials from the Warner library of the Wisconsin Center for Film and Theater Research were used by Dick in preparing *Dark Victory* for the Wisconsin/Warner Bros. Screenplay Series:

Play, by George Brewer, Jr., and Bertram Bloch. Typescript of January 8, 1936. 104 pages.
Screenplay, by Casey Robinson. July 1, 1938. Incomplete. 70 pages.
Outline, by Robinson, Edmund Goulding, and David Lewis. July 20, 1938. 36 pages.
Screenplay, by Robinson. No date. 185 pages.
Temporary, by Robinson. September 27 with revisions to September 28, 1938. 153 pages.
Final, by Robinson. September 27 with revisions to December 3, 1938. 160 pages.

DESIGNED BY GARY GORE
COMPOSED BY THE NORTH CENTRAL PUBLISHING COMPANY
ST. PAUL, MINNESOTA
MANUFACTURED BY INTER-COLLEGIATE PRESS, INC.
SHAWNEE MISSION, KANSAS
TEXT AND DISPLAY LINES ARE SET IN PALATINO

Library of Congress Cataloging in Publication Data
Robinson, Casey.
Dark victory.
(Wisconsin/Warner Bros. screenplay series)
"Screenplay by Casey Robinson from the play
by George Brewer, Jr. and Bertram Bloch"
I. Dick, Bernard F.
II. Brewer, George, 1899–1968. Dark victory.
III. Wisconsin Center for Film and Theater Research.
IV. Title.   V. Series.
PN1997.D314   1981   791.43′72   81-50822
ISBN 0-299-08760-3   AACR2
ISBN 0-299-08764-6 (pbk.)

WISCONSIN/WARNER BROS SCREENPLAY SERIES

The Wisconsin/Warner Bros. Screenplay Series, a product of the Warner Brothers Film Library of the University of Wisconsin-Madison, offers scholars, students, researchers, and aficionados insights into individual films that have never before been possible.

The Warner library was acquired in 1957 by the United Artists Corporation, which in turn donated it to the Wisconsin Center for Film and Theater Research in 1969. The massive library, housed in the State Historical Society of Wisconsin, contains eight hundred sound feature films, fifteen hundred short subjects, and nineteen thousand still negatives, as well as the legal files, press books, and screenplays of virtually every Warner film produced from 1930 until 1950. This rich treasure trove has made the University of Wisconsin one of the major centers for film research, attracting scholars from around the world. This series of published screenplays represents a creative use of the Warner library, both a boon to scholars and a tribute to United Artists.

Most published film scripts are literal transcriptions of finished films. The Wisconsin/Warner screenplays are primary source documents—the final shooting versions including revisions made during production. As such, they reveal the art of screenwriting as other film transcriptions cannot. Comparing these screenplays with the final films will illuminate the arts of directing and acting, as well as the other arts of the film making process. (Films of the Warner library are available at modest rates from the United Artists nontheatrical rental library, United Artists/16 mm.)

From the eight hundred feature films in the library, the editors of the series selected for publication examples that have received critical recognition for excellence of directing, screenwriting, and acting, films distinctive in genre, in historical relevance, and in adaptation of well-known novels and plays.